Unveiling the Shadows: Decoding the Signs of Cult Affiliations

Unveiling the Shadows: Decoding the Signs of Cult Affiliations

Decoding the Signs of Cult Affiliations

Armani Colt

Bald and Bonkers Network LLC

CONTENTS

One | Introduction to Cult Affiliations   1

Two | Signs of a Cult   12

Three | Signs of a Religious Cult   27

Four | Signs of a Political Cult   49

Five | Signs of a Conspiracy Theory Cult   68

Six | Signs of a Spiritual Cult   84

Seven | Signs of a New Age Cult   103

CONTENTS

Eight | Signs of a Celebrity or
Fanatical Following Cult 116

Nine | Recovery and Support 136

Ten | Shedding Light on Cult
Affiliations 154

One

Introduction to Cult Affiliations

Understanding Cults

Cults have, throughout history, maintained an enigmatic allure that has intrigued scholars and the broader public. This subchapter embarks on a comprehensive exploration of the intricate world of cults, peeling back the layers to reveal the cryptic signs that characterize them and shedding light on their diverse manifestations. Whether you find yourself contemplating potential cult affiliations or are a true crime enthusiast seeking a deeper understanding, this chapter promises to provide invaluable insights into the myriad forms of cults and their distinguishing features.

Let's delve even deeper into the fundamental signs that serve as breadcrumbs leading individuals through the labyrinth of cult involvement. These signs include charismatic leaders, deliberate isolation from mainstream society, manipulative control tactics, and an unwavering devotion to the group's doctrines. By comprehending these markers, individuals can discern whether they are ensnared in a cult or have unwittingly crossed paths with one.

Our exploration extends to the realm of religious cults, one of the most prevalent manifestations. We scrutinize the nuanced signs that differentiate a religious group from a religious cult, exploring facets such as the manipulation of scripture, the adoption of extreme beliefs, and the emergence of a dominant leader who claims divine authority. Through this meticulous examination, readers cultivate a profound understanding of the subtle boundary between genuine religious devotion and cult affiliation.

Moreover, our journey takes us through the terrain of political cults, conspiracy theory cults, spiritual cults, and new age cults. Each of these cult types possesses unique characteristics and signs that will be unveiled, empowering readers to identify potential cult affiliations within these diverse niches. From the grandiose proclamations of political cult leaders to the mystique surrounding esoteric spiritual practices, we uncover the multifaceted tactics employed by these cults to manipulate and exert control over their adherents.

A fascinating aspect of our exploration is the revelation of celebrity or fanatical following cults. In an era dominated by social media and the cult of personality, individuals often develop obsessive and unhealthy attachments to public figures. By unraveling the signs indicative of these celebrity cults, readers gain profound insights into the hazards and dynamics inherent in such relationships.

In conclusion, this subchapter stands as a comprehensive guide, illuminating the shadows of cult psychology and deciphering the myriad manifestations of cults. By unraveling the signs of cult affiliations within religious, political, conspiracy theory, spiritual, new age, and celebrity cults, readers find themselves better armed to protect against the manipulative tactics employed by these groups. Whether seeking personal clarity or driven by sheer intrigue into the world of cults, "Unveiling the Shadows: Decoding the Signs of Cult Affiliations" promises an enlightening journey into the intricate landscape of cult psychology.

The Impact of Cults on Individuals and Society

Cults, with their insidious influence, leave an indelible mark on both individuals and society at large. This subchapter aims to delve even deeper into the myriad ways in which cults wield their influence over individuals and explore the broader implications they cast upon society.

For those grappling with the realization of potential cult affiliations, a nuanced understanding of the signs and characteristics of cults becomes paramount. Cults, as master manipulators, employ a repertoire of psychological tactics, isolation techniques, and the exploitation of vulnerability to assert control over their members. The consequences are profound, resulting in a gradual erosion of personal identity, compromised critical thinking abilities, and a warped perception of reality.

Individuals ensnared in the clutches of cults often bear the brunt of a spectrum of adverse effects. From emotional and psychological trauma to financial exploitation and, in extreme cases, physical harm, the toll is extensive. Cult leaders, wielding coercive tactics, strip followers of autonomy, leaving them ensnared in a web of control. Recognizing these telltale signs of cult involvement becomes imperative for those yearning to reclaim their autonomy and extricate themselves from the pervasive influence of these organizations.

The repercussions of cults transcend the

individual realm, extending their tentacles to grasp society as a whole. Cults wield a destructive influence on social cohesion, systematically isolating their members from friends, family, and mainstream society. This isolation often precipitates the unraveling of relationships and community ties, leaving individuals stranded in a desolate landscape of alienation.

Moreover, certain genres of cults, such as political or conspiracy theory cults, emerge as potential threats to democratic values and social stability. These groups, fueled by extremist ideologies and the perpetuation of conspiracy theories, embark on radicalization efforts that can corrode the fabric of society. The resultant division and polarization sow seeds of distrust, threatening the democratic process and undermining societal harmony.

The digital age has ushered in a new era, amplifying the impact of cults. Online platforms serve as fertile ground for cult recruitment and the dissemination of their ideologies. Individuals susceptible to cult influence find themselves drawn into echo chambers that reinforce their beliefs while isolating them further from dissenting viewpoints.

For aficionados of true crime, delving into the impact of cults provides a glimpse into the shadowy recesses of society. By dissecting the signs of a cult and comprehending its effects on individuals and society, true crime enthusiasts can unravel the motivations and tactics employed by cult leaders. This knowledge, in turn, contributes to a collective effort to raise awareness, prevent future cult involvement, and extend support to those grappling with the aftermath of cult experiences.

In conclusion, the impact of cults on individuals and society is profound and intricate. By acknowledging the signs of a cult and unraveling their methods of control, individuals can take proactive steps to safeguard themselves and liberate themselves from the clutches of cult influence. Additionally, society must remain vigilant to the menace posed by cults, recognizing their potential to erode social cohesion, democratic values, and personal freedom.

The Need for Unveiling the Shadows

In a world where the quest for meaning and belonging is ceaseless, the alluring yet perilous embrace of cults cannot be overlooked. Cult affiliations, whether religious, political, conspiracy theory-based, spiritual, new age, or centered around celebrity or fanatical followings, manifest in diverse and subtle forms. The escalating prevalence of cults demands our attention, underscoring the critical need to shed light on the signs and dangers associated with these enigmatic and clandestine organizations.

The subchapter titled "The Need for Unveiling the Shadows" is designed to meticulously explore the reasons why it is not just important but imperative to expose and understand cult affiliations. Tailored specifically for individuals who harbor suspicions of cult affiliations and true crime enthusiasts eager to unravel the intricacies of these covert groups, this section serves as a beacon guiding them through the labyrinth of cult psychology.

One of the paramount reasons for unveiling the

shadows lies in the imperative to safeguard individuals who may unknowingly find themselves ensnared within these clandestine organizations. The initial attraction to cults often stems from a genuine search for purpose, community, and a sense of belonging. However, what may commence as an apparently innocuous association can swiftly metamorphose into a hazardous and manipulative environment. By honing the ability to identify the subtle signs indicative of a cult, individuals can gain the crucial awareness needed to extricate themselves from the potential harms lurking within these groups.

Furthermore, the significance of understanding the signs of diverse types of cult affiliations extends to the societal level. Through the meticulous decoding of the signs exhibited by religious, political, conspiracy theory, spiritual, new age, and celebrity-based cults, we empower ourselves to recognize and address the underlying societal issues that give rise to their formation. Armed with this knowledge, we can proactively work towards protecting vulnerable individuals and curbing the proliferation of harmful ideologies that have the potential to inflict detrimental effects on both individuals and communities.

For aficionados of true crime, "The Need for Unveiling the Shadows" offers an unparalleled journey into the intricate psychology and dynamics that underpin these secretive organizations. Through the exploration of real-life examples and detailed case studies, readers gain a profound understanding of the insidious tactics employed by cult leaders to manipulate and control their followers. This knowledge becomes a potent tool in the arsenal of prevention and investigation of cult-related crimes, ensuring that justice is served and potential victims are shielded from harm.

In conclusion, within the framework of the book "Unveiling the Shadows: Decoding the Signs of Cult Affiliations," the subchapter titled "The Need for Unveiling the Shadows" emerges as an indispensable resource. It not only serves as a guiding light for individuals grappling with suspicions of cult affiliations but also stands as an invaluable resource for true crime enthusiasts. By shining a light on the signs and dangers inherent in various types of cults, this subchapter empowers readers to navigate the shadows and protect themselves and others from the perils posed by these secretive organizations.

Two

Signs of a Cult

Definition and Characteristics of a Cult

In the realm of psychology and social phenomena, the term "cult" has been a subject of both confusion and controversy. This subchapter seeks to demystify the concept of a cult by providing a clear definition and exploring its key characteristics. By understanding the signs and attributes of a cult, individuals who suspect they may have cult affiliations can gain valuable insights, while true crime enthusiasts can deepen their knowledge of these intriguing groups.

Defining a Cult:

A cult can be defined as a group or organization

exhibiting several key characteristics. These typically include:

1. Charismatic Leader:

- A cult often has a charismatic leader who exerts significant influence over its followers. This leader is typically perceived as extraordinary or divine, and their words carry immense weight within the group.

2. Tightly Knit and Exclusive Community:

- Cults tend to form a tightly knit and exclusive community. Members may isolate themselves from mainstream society, creating a distinct social environment that reinforces the group's identity.

3. Deviation from Norms:

- Cults usually adhere to belief systems that deviate significantly from the norms and values of mainstream society. These beliefs may be unconventional, extreme, or unorthodox.

Signs of Cults in Different Domains:

1. Religious Cults:

- Authoritarian Leader: Cults in the religious domain often have an authoritarian leader who claims divine revelation and demands unwavering loyalty.

- Manipulative Tactics: They employ manipulative tactics and may isolate members from external influences, fostering dependency.

2. Political Cults:

- Charismatic Leader: Political cults revolve around a charismatic leader manipulating followers' political ideologies.

- Echo Chamber: Isolation from opposing viewpoints creates an echo chamber reinforcing the leader's agenda.

3. Conspiracy Theory Cults:

- Alternative Narratives: Thriving on alternative narratives, conspiracy theory cults reject mainstream information.

- Strong Us-Versus-Them Mentality: Cult members exhibit a strong us-versus-them mentality, fostering paranoia and distrust.

4. Spiritual and New Age Cults:

- Self-Improvement Focus: Spiritual and new age cults focus on self-improvement and personal transformation.

- Unconventional Practices: They may incorporate spirituality, pseudoscience, or unconventional practices to attract followers.

5. Celebrity or Fanatical Followings:

- Idolization: Celebrity cults involve extreme idolization of a particular figure, with fans forming a community around their idol.

- Extreme Behaviors: Individuals within these cults may engage in extreme behaviors, such as stalking or violence, to protect and support their chosen celebrity.

By acquainting themselves with the signs and characteristics of cults, individuals can gain clarity and understanding regarding potential cult affiliations. This knowledge is crucial for safeguarding against harm and manipulation. Additionally, true crime enthusiasts can benefit from a deeper comprehension of these intriguing and often dangerous groups. Recognizing the signs and understanding the dynamics of cults is a crucial step in promoting awareness and protection.

Introduction to Psychological Manipulation in Cults

In the shadowy realms of society, cults utilize psychological manipulation to exploit vulnerable individuals, preying on their hopes, fears, and desires. This subchapter explores the intricate workings of mind control techniques employed by cults, shedding light on the signs and strategies that enable these organizations to gain control over their followers' minds.

Cults, regardless of their specific objectives or forms—be they religious, political, conspiracy-driven, spiritual, new age, or centered around celebrity worship—rely on consistent underlying mechanisms of manipulation. These include isolation, charismatic leadership, mind control techniques, fear and guilt induction, and the enforcement of rigid rules. Understanding these tactics is crucial for individuals who suspect cult affiliations, as well as for the general public, including true crime enthusiasts.

Isolation: The Power to Control

Isolation serves as one of the most potent tools in a cult's arsenal. By cutting off contact with the outside world, cult leaders create an environment where their ideology reigns supreme. The absence of dissenting voices within the group effectively stifles critical thinking, making followers more susceptible to manipulation.

Cult leaders discourage or even forbid contact with family and friends outside the group, fostering a closed system where information flows exclusively through the cult. Dissenting opinions are shunned, and the isolation serves to create a sense of exclusive belonging and dependency on the cult for social interaction, emotional support, and validation.

Understanding the signs of isolation is crucial for those caught in the web of a cult. If you find yourself cut off from loved ones, restricted from engaging with different perspectives, or feeling a constant need for validation from the group, these may be signs of unhealthy isolation.

Dependency: The Shackles of Loyalty

Dependency is another tactic employed by cults to ensure unwavering loyalty and control. Cult leaders often position themselves as all-knowing or divine figures, claiming exclusive access to spiritual truths or hidden knowledge. They exploit vulnerabilities, manipulate emotions, and instill a deep sense of dependency on the cult and its leaders.

Members are made to feel incapable of making decisions or living fulfilling lives without the guidance and approval of the cult. The fear of ostracism or punishment keeps individuals tightly bound to the group's teachings and rules.

Recognizing signs of dependency is challenging, but it's crucial for breaking free from the grip of a cult. If you feel unable to make decisions without cult approval, or if your sense of self is entirely tied to the group's ideology, these may be indications of unhealthy dependency.

Breaking Free: Reclaiming Autonomy

Escaping the clutches of a cult requires recognizing the signs of isolation and dependency and taking active steps to reclaim one's autonomy. Seeking support from trusted friends, family members, or professionals who can provide a fresh perspective is essential. Educating oneself about the tactics used by cults and understanding the signs of manipulation is a powerful tool in breaking free.

Remember, you are not alone, and there is a way out of the isolation and dependency fostered by cult affiliations. By shedding light on these tactics, this subchapter aims to empower individuals to recognize the warning signs and take the necessary steps to break free from the insidious influence of cults. In the subsequent sections, we will delve deeper into specific mind control techniques and their impact on individuals caught in the web of cult affiliations.

Financial Exploitation: Unraveling the Dark Threads

In the clandestine world of cult affiliations, financial exploitation emerges as a particularly insidious weapon wielded by charismatic leaders masquerading as spiritual or political guides. Within the shadows, vulnerable individuals seeking meaning, purpose, or belonging fall prey to the manipulative tactics that cult leaders employ to maintain control and further their own agendas.

The signs of financial exploitation within cults manifest in multifaceted ways, weaving a complex web of deception. A common ploy involves the demand for exorbitant donations or tithes, cunningly disguised as contributions to the cult's mission or pathways to spiritual enlightenment. Believers find themselves coerced into relinquishing their hard-earned money, sometimes even sacrificing life savings, in a bid to maintain their status within the group or gain access to promised rewards.

Beyond this, cult leaders cunningly establish income-generating schemes that primarily serve their own interests. These schemes may take the form of pyramid structures, multi-level marketing programs, or even fraudulent business ventures. Followers are ensnared by the illusion that participation in these endeavors is crucial for their spiritual growth or to contribute to the cult's purported objectives. However, the stark reality is that these schemes function as conduits to enrich the leader, perpetuating their control over the group.

To tighten their grip further, cult leaders manipulate followers into severing ties with skeptical family and friends. This isolation tactic, while ostensibly eliminating external influences, serves a dual purpose by weakening the support network that could potentially aid members in recognizing and escaping the financial exploitation they endure.

Recognizing the signs of financial exploitation within a cult is not just a matter of financial prudence; it is a lifeline for those ensnared in the clutches of cult affiliations. Drastic financial changes, such as unexplained bankruptcy or accumulating excessive debt, should act as red flags prompting individuals to question their involvement. Equally significant is the recognition of feeling pressured or coerced into making financial contributions that contradict one's best interests —an unmistakable sign of financial exploitation.

For true crime enthusiasts, understanding the signs of financial exploitation within cults becomes a key to unraveling the methods employed by these manipulative leaders. By exposing these tactics, society can build a shield to better protect vulnerable individuals from falling victim to the insidious financial schemes devised by cult leaders.

Whether the cult takes on the guise of religious, political, conspiracy theory, spiritual, new age, or celebrity affiliations, the signs of financial exploitation persist with alarming consistency. Through empowerment via knowledge and awareness, "Unveiling the Shadows: Decoding the Signs of Cult Affiliations" endeavors to expose the dark underpinnings of cults. By providing a roadmap for those seeking liberation from the grip of financial exploitation, it aspires to guide individuals towards breaking free from the shadows that threaten to engulf them.

Charismatic Leaders and Devotion: Navigating the Labyrinth of Influence

In the realm of cult affiliations, charismatic leaders wield an unparalleled influence, drawing followers into their orbit with charm, eloquence, and persuasive abilities. These magnetic figures possess an innate understanding of human desires and vulnerabilities, presenting themselves as saviors offering a better future, spiritual enlightenment, or a sense of belonging. Understanding the intricate dynamics between charismatic leaders and the unwavering devotion they inspire is fundamental to decoding the signs of cult affiliations.

The allure of charismatic leaders is particularly potent for those who feel lost, disillusioned, or yearning for meaning in their lives. These leaders emerge as beacons of hope, promising fulfillment of deep-seated desires and needs. The key sign of a cult lies in the undying devotion exhibited by followers towards these leaders—an allegiance that transcends mere loyalty and often transforms into blind obedience.

Religious cults harness charismatic leaders to manipulate people's faith and spirituality, gaining control by distorting interpretations of sacred texts and exaggerating claims of divine authority. In this context, charismatic figures manipulate the inherent human need for spirituality, using it as a tool to control and exploit vulnerable individuals.

Political cults, on the other hand, rely on charismatic leaders who promise revolutionary change or utopian ideals. Capitalizing on people's frustrations, fears, and desires for societal improvement, these leaders create an atmosphere of unquestioning loyalty. Followers willingly sacrifice their beliefs and values, placing the leader's cause above all else.

Conspiracy theory cults revolve around charismatic leaders claiming possession of secret knowledge or hidden truths. Targeting those disillusioned with mainstream society, these leaders create a sense of exclusivity and encourage blind devotion by presenting themselves as the sole bearers of truth.

New age and spiritual cults exploit the human desire for personal growth and fulfillment. Charismatic leaders present themselves as enlightened beings, offering followers the keys to transcendence and self-realization. The intense devotion exhibited by followers in these cults is rooted in the belief that the leader holds the key to their spiritual awakening.

Celebrity or fanatical following cults center around charismatic leaders who exploit their fame and influence to attract followers. These leaders, often possessing a cult of personality, are idolized and emulated to an extreme degree. The devotion shown by followers in these cults goes to great lengths, as individuals seek attention and approval from their idol.

Understanding these dynamics is pivotal in

decoding the signs of cult affiliations. The patterns of blind loyalty, unquestioning obedience, and idolization serve as red flags, signaling potential danger. Cult affiliations, regardless of their guise—religious, political, conspiracy theory, spiritual, new age, or celebrity-driven—rely on charismatic leaders to ensnare followers in their web of influence. Recognizing this influence is the first step toward liberation from the shadows of cult affiliations.

By fostering awareness and understanding, individuals can shield themselves and others from falling prey to the seductive charisma of cult leaders. "Unveiling the Shadows: Decoding the Signs of Cult Affiliations" strives to illuminate these patterns, empowering individuals to break free from the clutches of dangerous cults and regain control over their lives. Awareness, indeed, serves as the beacon guiding those ensnared towards the path of liberation.

Three

Signs of a Religious Cult

Navigating the Complex Terrain: Differentiating Between Religion and Cult

In our contemporary and intricate world, the challenge of distinguishing between genuine religious beliefs and the perilous allure of a cult has become increasingly complex. While religions often offer solace, guidance, and a sense of community, the manipulative tendencies of cults can lead vulnerable individuals down a path of lasting harm. To safeguard oneself and loved ones, a profound understanding of the distinct characteristics that set apart a religion from a cult is crucial.

Religions typically find their roots in ancient traditions, boasting a rich and established history. Often accompanied by sacred texts or scriptures like the Bible or the Quran, they provide moral guidelines and teachings that encourage followers to question and seek spiritual enlightenment through personal faith. On the contrary, cults tend to emerge more recently and lack the historical depth found in traditional religions. They may be characterized by charismatic leaders who assert exclusive knowledge or divine connections, demanding unwavering obedience from their adherents.

A pivotal divergence between religions and cults lies in their attitude towards critical thinking. Religions generally foster an environment where believers are encouraged to question, engage in debates, and interpret teachings based on their individual understanding. In stark contrast, cults actively discourage critical thinking, imposing a rigid ideology that must be accepted without question. Cult leaders frequently employ mind control techniques, isolating followers from external influences and enforcing stringent rules to maintain unquestioning loyalty.

Another vital aspect to consider is the degree of control exerted by religious institutions versus cults. Religions commonly provide a spectrum of choices, allowing adherents to determine their level of involvement. These belief systems respect personal autonomy and freedom, enabling individuals to practice their faith as they deem fit. On the flip side, cults resort to coercive tactics, extending control over every facet of their followers' lives. This control extends beyond religious practices, encompassing financial exploitation, isolation from friends and family, and even instances of physical abuse.

Moreover, religions typically emphasize the well-being of their followers and society at large. Core values such as love, compassion, and charity are championed, encouraging adherents to contribute positively to their communities. In contrast, cults often prioritize the personal interests and goals of their leaders above all else. Followers may be exploited for personal gain or manipulated to achieve specific, and at times harmful, objectives.

Understanding these nuanced distinctions empowers individuals to recognize the signs of cult affiliations and shields them from potential harm. Whether one is a true crime enthusiast or someone grappling with the suspicion of cult affiliations, remaining vigilant and well-informed about these warning signs becomes paramount. The ability to distinguish between a religion and a cult is an empowering tool, aiding individuals in making informed decisions on their spiritual journey and avoiding the snares of manipulative and abusive organizations.

"Unveiling the Shadows: Decoding the Signs of Cult Affiliations" stands as an indispensable resource for those navigating the complexities of cult dynamics, offering insights that serve as a shield against potential harm.

Unraveling the Layers: The Distorted Interpretation of Scripture in Cult Dynamics

Within the intricate realm of cult affiliations, few tools wield as much power to manipulate and control followers as the distorted interpretation of scripture. This subchapter delves into the profound implications of this practice, shedding light on the disturbing techniques employed by cult leaders and providing insight for individuals to recognize the signs of cults utilizing such tactics.

Religious cults, notorious for their adeptness at distorting scripture, often prey on vulnerable individuals seeking spiritual guidance and meaning in their lives. Through selective interpretation of passages, cult leaders craft a narrative convincing followers that they alone possess exclusive access to divine knowledge, and their teachings represent the sole path to salvation. This manipulation often results in a complete surrender of critical thinking, fostering blind obedience to the cult's doctrine.

Remarkably, the distortion of scripture is not

confined to religious cults alone. Political cults, conspiracy theory cults, spiritual cults, new age cults, and even celebrity or fanatical following cults can seamlessly employ this insidious tactic. By twisting religious texts or repurposing them to support their own ideologies, these cults establish a veneer of legitimacy and authority that proves challenging for followers to question.

Recognizing the signs of a cult employing scripture distortion is paramount for those who suspect their involvement in such affiliations. Common indicators include:

1. Selective Quoting and Interpretation: Cult leaders often cherry-pick verses that align with their beliefs, conveniently sidelining contradictory passages to fortify their narrative.

2. Absolute Authority over Interpretation: Cult leaders claim exclusive interpretative authority, dissuading followers from seeking alternative perspectives or engaging in independent study.

3. Manipulation of Fear and Guilt: Distorted interpretations are used to instill fear and guilt in followers, further tightening the leader's control and fostering dependency.

4. Suppression of Critical Thinking: Followers are actively discouraged from questioning the cult's teachings or logically analyzing scriptures, reinforcing the leader's authoritarian hold.

Understanding these signs empowers individuals to break free from the clutches of distorted scripture interpretations. Seeking support from professionals, engaging in open dialogue with trusted friends or family members, and educating oneself about diverse interpretations are crucial steps toward reclaiming autonomy and breaking free from the influence of cult affiliations.

In conclusion, the distorted interpretation of scripture stands as a potent weapon in the arsenal of cult leaders for manipulating and controlling their followers. Recognizing the signs of this manipulation is not only essential for those suspecting cult affiliations but serves as a critical step toward regaining control of beliefs and embarking on a journey toward healing and freedom.

As individuals unravel the layers of manipulation, they pave the way for a future grounded in self-discovery and autonomy.

Navigating the Shadows: The Pervasive Influence of Excessive Control in Cult Dynamics

In the enigmatic realm of cult affiliations, few aspects are as alarming and profoundly impactful as the excessive control exerted over the lives of followers. This expansive exploration, encapsulated within the subchapter of "Unveiling the Shadows: Decoding the Signs of Cult Affiliations," delves into the multifaceted manifestations of this disturbing phenomenon and illuminates its devastating effects on individuals ensnared in its grip.

Cult leaders, whether they emerge from religious, political, conspiracy theory, spiritual, new age, or celebrity followings, share a common objective—to manipulate and dominate their followers through an unwavering control over every facet of their lives. This subchapter unveils the insidious ways in which this control unfolds, revealing a series of manipulative tactics employed by cult leaders.

At the forefront of these tactics is the utilization of mind control techniques, strategically designed to shape and manipulate the thoughts and beliefs of followers. The cult environment becomes a breeding ground where independent thinking is not only discouraged but forbidden, and blind loyalty becomes the sole acceptable path. This mental manipulation strips individuals of their autonomy, rendering them susceptible to the pervasive influence of the leader's suggestions.

Beyond the realm of thought manipulation, cult leaders establish a regime of strict rules and regulations dictating every nuance of their followers' lives. From the intricacies of daily routines to the complexities of personal relationships, and from pivotal financial decisions to career choices, no aspect remains untouched by the far-reaching arm of the leader's control. Exploiting the vulnerabilities and fears of their followers, cult leaders maintain a vice-like grip over every facet of their lives.

Isolation, another potent weapon in the arsenal of manipulative leaders, serves to sever the ties between followers and the outside world. By creating an environment where dissenting voices are silenced, these leaders make it increasingly difficult for individuals to escape their clutches. This isolation not only reinforces the leader's control but also acts as a formidable barrier, preventing followers from seeking help or support from friends and family who may question the cult's practices.

The consequences of such excessive control over followers' lives are profound and far-reaching, leading to the erosion of an individual's sense of self, personal agency, and ability to make rational decisions. Complete dependency on the cult and its leader often results in severe psychological and emotional trauma, leaving an indelible mark on the lives of those ensnared.

Recognizing the signs of excessive control is

paramount for individuals who suspect they may be entangled in cult affiliations. This subchapter functions as a comprehensive guide, shedding light on the warning signs and providing crucial insights to help individuals break free from the clutches of these manipulative cults.

For true crime enthusiasts, this exploration serves as an eye-opening journey into the tactics employed by cult leaders to control and exploit their followers. Understanding these manipulative tactics offers a deeper comprehension of the dark underbelly of cult affiliations, fostering awareness to prevent their insidious influence on vulnerable individuals.

In conclusion, the knowledge encapsulated within the decoding of signs associated with cult affiliations is a powerful tool. It is through this understanding that we can hope to unveil the shadows that obscure the truth, empowering individuals to navigate the complexities of cult dynamics and reclaim their autonomy in the process.

Unraveling the Veil: The Devastating Impact of Isolation in Cult Dynamics

Within the intricate tapestry of cult affiliations, few tactics are as prevalent and perilous as the isolation of followers from nonbelievers. This expansive exploration, encapsulated in this subchapter, delves into the nuanced ways in which cults manipulate their members, severing ties with friends, family, and the external world—a stark signal of cult affiliation that demands our attention.

Cult leaders, well-versed in the art of psychological manipulation, recognize isolation as a potent tool for controlling their followers. The deliberate cutoff from communication with nonbelievers compels cult members to become entirely reliant on the group for social interactions, emotional sustenance, and the very definition of their identity. This isolation is cunningly masked as a protective measure against perceived threats from the outside world—be it the alleged corruption of mainstream society or the skepticism of nonbelievers.

In the realm of religious cults, isolation is often

justified as a means to uphold purity and shield followers from the influence of those who do not share the same faith. Associating with nonbelievers is framed as a sin or a form of spiritual contamination, reinforcing the walls around the cult's belief system. Similarly, political cults employ isolation to insulate their members from opposing ideologies, fostering a sense of superiority and fortifying the cult's convictions.

Conspiracy theory cults take isolation a step further by propagating the notion that nonbelievers are part of a grand conspiracy to suppress the truth. The isolationist strategy creates an echo chamber where dissenting opinions are not only discouraged but forbidden, facilitating easier manipulation and control over followers.

In the realm of spiritual and new age cults, the manipulation leverages vulnerability and a quest for spiritual enlightenment. Members are persuaded that nonbelievers lack the profound spiritual understanding they have attained, rationalizing the necessity of isolation. Celebrity or fanatical following cults prompt members to isolate themselves from nonbelievers to preserve a sense of exclusivity and unwavering devotion to their idol.

The peril of isolation from nonbelievers lies in its power to sever access to alternative perspectives and critical thinking. It constructs an environment where questioning the beliefs and actions of the group is actively discouraged and may even be met with punishment. This subchapter endeavors to illuminate this insidious technique, offering a beacon to individuals to recognize the signs of isolation as a clear warning of cult affiliation.

For those suspecting their involvement in a cult, comprehension of the manipulative methods employed is imperative. Armed with this knowledge, individuals can embark on a journey to break free from the suffocating grip of isolation, seeking solace and support from friends, family, or professional organizations dedicated to cult recovery.

True crime enthusiasts, drawn to the enigmatic

allure of cult dynamics, will find this subchapter an enthralling exploration. It unveils the psychological tactics employed by cults to control and manipulate their followers, providing a profound understanding of the intricate inner workings and the profound impact they leave on their victims.

In conclusion, isolation from nonbelievers stands as a glaring red flag for cult affiliation. Recognition of this tactic empowers individuals to shield themselves and their loved ones from the deleterious influence of cults, offering a pathway toward resilience and liberation from the shadows that obscure the truth.

Unveiling the Enigma: The Profound Impact of Sacrifice and Ritualistic Practices in Cult Dynamics

In the realm of cult affiliations, sacrifice and ritualistic practices cast a profound and enigmatic shadow. These practices, often veiled in secrecy and mystique, exert a powerful allure that draws individuals into the intricate web of cults. This expansive subchapter endeavors to illuminate the intricacies of sacrifices and rituals, unraveling their signs and deciphering their implications.

Sacrifice, a term resonating with images of ancient rituals, blood offerings, and unwavering devotion, persists in various forms within modern cults. Despite their seemingly archaic nature, these practices continue to wield influence, necessitating an understanding of their signs to navigate the treacherous depths of cult affiliations.

On the other hand, ritualistic practices within cult dynamics encompass a diverse spectrum. Ranging from simple ceremonies and repetitive actions to elaborate rites involving chanting, dancing, and mind-altering substances, these practices provide a lens through which to comprehend the extent of control exerted by cult leaders over their followers.

A distinctive sign of cult affiliation lies in the incorporation of sacrifices or offerings as a means of demonstrating devotion or loyalty. Cult leaders adeptly manipulate their followers, coaxing them into acts that defy societal norms, using these acts as litmus tests for loyalty and commitment. These sacrifices may transcend mere material possessions, encompassing personal relationships or even venturing into the realm of physical harm.

Another notable sign is the utilization of rituals to forge a profound sense of belonging and identity within the cult. Serving as a potent tool for indoctrination, rituals reinforce the group's ideology, nurturing a collective mindset. Through repetitive actions, symbolism, and communal experiences, cults solidify their members' commitment while suppressing individuality.

It is imperative to acknowledge that not all rituals and sacrifices are inherently harmful or indicative of cult affiliations. Many mainstream religious and spiritual practices incorporate rituals as mechanisms for fostering connection and personal growth. However, when these practices are wielded as tools for manipulation, control, or harm, they morph into clear signs of potential cult affiliation.

"Unveiling the Shadows: Decoding the Signs of Cult Affiliations" aspires to arm individuals with the knowledge necessary to discern signs of cult involvement. By delving into the intricate world of sacrifices and ritualistic practices, this subchapter seeks to empower readers to identify red flags and make informed decisions about their beliefs and affiliations.

For those grappling with the suspicion of cult affiliations, this subchapter serves as a guide, providing valuable insights into the manipulative tactics employed by cult leaders. It serves as a starting point for self-reflection and understanding, offering a pathway for individuals to evaluate their experiences and seek assistance if needed.

True crime enthusiasts will find this subchapter particularly captivating as it plunges into the darker facets of cult dynamics. By decoding the signs of sacrifice and ritualistic practices, it provides a riveting exploration into the psychology underpinning cult affiliations and the intricate power dynamics at play.

Lastly, for those intrigued by the diverse niches of cult affiliations, spanning religious, political, conspiracy theory, spiritual, new age, and celebrity/fanatical followings, this subchapter furnishes a comprehensive overview of signs specific to each niche. It serves as an invaluable resource for comprehending the subtle nuances and distinct characteristics inherent in different cult affiliations.

In summation, sacrifice and ritualistic practices wield substantial influence within cult affiliations. Through the decoding of their signs and implications, this subchapter serves as a guide, assisting individuals in identifying red flags, understanding the psychology intrinsic to cult dynamics, and making informed decisions about their beliefs and affiliations.

Navigating the Depths: Exclusive

Salvation and the Intricacies of Judgmental Beliefs in Cult Dynamics

Within the intricate tapestry of cult affiliations, a recurring theme unfurls — the pervasive notion of exclusive salvation coupled with the presence of judgmental beliefs. These twin pillars play a pivotal role in shaping the dynamics within cults, and a comprehensive understanding of these elements is indispensable for individuals grappling with suspected cult affiliations or for the discerning gaze of true crime enthusiasts.

Exclusive salvation, a concept entrenched in the belief that only an elite few hold the ultimate truth or salvation, while the rest are consigned to doom or deemed inferior, establishes a framework of superiority and exclusion. Within this paradigm, cult members are persuaded that they alone possess the key to enlightenment or salvation, casting everyone beyond their chosen circle as misguided or lost. This exclusivity reverberates across a spectrum of cults, spanning the religious, political, conspiracy theory, and spiritual domains.

The signs of exclusive salvation manifest diversely. In religious cults, proclamations may echo that only the cult's interpretation of scripture or doctrine paves the way to salvation, condemning all alternative belief systems. Political cults might assert that only their ideology heralds societal change, dismissing alternative viewpoints as ignorant or perilous. Similarly, spiritual and new age cults could avow that their specific practices or teachings exclusively usher in spiritual awakening, dismissing other paths as ineffectual or inferior.

Hand in hand with exclusive salvation often walks a set of judgmental beliefs. Cult members are systematically conditioned to perceive the outside world as flawed, misguided, or even malevolent. This judgmental mindset begets a sense of isolation from society, fortifying the cult's control over its members. Leaders deftly manipulate followers by instilling fear and paranoia, weaving a narrative that they alone comprehend the world's truths, with everyone else cast as a potential threat or enemy.

Recognizing the signs of exclusive salvation and judgmental beliefs is of paramount importance for those suspecting cult involvement or for true crime enthusiasts seeking insights into the intricate dynamics of cult affiliations. Armed with an understanding of these factors, individuals can initiate the unraveling of the psychological manipulation at play, taking measured steps toward reclaiming their autonomy and freedom of thought.

In the forthcoming chapters, we embark on a detailed exploration of each cult affiliation type, meticulously unveiling the specific signs and red flags associated with religious, political, conspiracy theory, spiritual, new age, and celebrity or fanatical following cults. Through the decoding of these signs, we aspire to empower individuals to discern the presence of exclusive salvation and judgmental beliefs, ultimately guiding them toward liberation from the shadows of cult affiliations. The journey ahead promises illumination and empowerment, offering a beacon of knowledge to navigate the intricate complexities woven into the fabric of cult dynamics.

Four

Signs of a Political Cult

Navigating the Nexus: Exploring the Intricate Relationship Between Politics and Cult Behavior

In the labyrinthine landscape of cult affiliations, a critical acknowledgment emerges — the profound intersection between politics and cult behavior. At their essence, cults are distinguished by a magnetic leader who deftly wields manipulative tactics to ensnare control over their followers. These leaders, with strategic cunning, often exploit political ideologies, whether overtly or covertly, to propel their agendas and entrench their dominion.

A glaring indicator of a political cult lies in the unwavering devotion and unquestioning fealty exhibited by its adherents towards a specific political figure or party. Within this realm, individuals showcase a fervent following akin to fanaticism, vehemently rebuffing any critique or dissent. The leader ascends to an almost divine stature, their proclamations treated as immutable truths. This blind obedience encapsulates a quintessential trait of cult behavior, serving to stifle critical thinking and suppress independent thought.

Conversely, conspiracy theory cults leverage political events and ideologies to foster a sense of exclusivity and superiority among their followers. Crafting narratives that portray themselves as the enlightened few privy to concealed knowledge about the world's intricate workings, these cults allure individuals disillusioned or marginalized by mainstream politics, offering a refuge of belonging and purpose.

The nexus between religious cults and politics

manifests when religious ideologies become instruments for gaining political sway or influence. These cults deftly manipulate their adherents, casting themselves as the chosen catalysts for a divine societal transformation. By aligning with political movements or parties, they coerce their members into championing their cause, often without a complete comprehension of their actions.

Moreover, the ascent of new age and spiritual cults blurs the demarcation between personal beliefs and political ideologies. These cults weave together spiritual practices and political activism, constructing a narrative of righteousness and moral ascendancy among their followers. Exploiting the quest for personal growth and enlightenment, they manipulate this pursuit as a tool for control, steering their members to support their political agenda.

In the arena of celebrity or fanatical following cults, political figures or celebrities become the epicenter of veneration and adulation. Exhibiting parallels with religious cults, these followings perceive their leader as a quasi-deity. Adherents idolize and emulate the leader, absorbing their political perspectives and advocating for their causes without question.

Grasping the intricacies of the intersection between politics and cult behavior is paramount for individuals grappling with perceived cult affiliations. Discerning the telltale signs of cult behavior within political contexts empowers individuals to liberate themselves from the clutches of manipulation and reclaim their autonomy. For true crime enthusiasts, delving into the dynamics of these cults unveils the shadowy underbelly of power and influence, offering insights into the labyrinth of human behavior and the vulnerabilities ripe for exploitation. The exploration of this nexus promises enlightenment, unraveling the complex tapestry woven by the interplay of politics and cult dynamics.

The Pillars of Conviction: Unraveling

Extreme Ideological Adherence in the Enigmatic World of Cults

Within the captivating tapestry of cults, extreme ideological adherence emerges as the bedrock upon which these clandestine communities are constructed. It is the magnetic force that binds individuals together, endowing them with a sense of belonging and purpose. Across the spectrum of religious, political, conspiracy theory, spiritual, new age, and celebrity-focused cults, the signs of extreme ideological adherence echo with remarkable similarity. By peeling back the layers of this phenomenon, we embark on a journey to grasp the allure and perils entwined with cult affiliations.

A salient hallmark of extreme ideological adherence manifests in the form of a rigid belief system, an ideological fortress that brooks no room for inquiry or skepticism. Cult members are meticulously indoctrinated to embrace a specific doctrine or ideology without reservation, often convinced that it represents the exclusive path to salvation, enlightenment, or societal metamorphosis. This unyielding commitment can be all-encompassing, compelling individuals to sever ties with friends, family, and the external world, ensnared in the labyrinth of their beliefs.

Another conspicuous sign of extreme ideological adherence materializes through the presence of charismatic leaders or figures wielding an extraordinary sway over their followers. Exploiting the vulnerabilities of their disciples, these leaders proffer answers to life's existential questions or proffer a sense of purpose and camaraderie. Their charisma and perceived authority exert such a magnetic pull that devotees willingly traverse extraordinary lengths, even to the point of sacrificing their own well-being, to advance the cult's mission.

In the realm of extreme ideological adherence, strict behavioral codes and rituals stand as visible markers. Members find themselves tethered to a set of stringent rules and regulations, often enforced through psychological manipulation or physical coercion. These codes dictate everything from attire and dietary habits to daily routines and interpersonal relationships. Straying from these prescribed norms invites severe repercussions, fortifying the cult's dominion over its adherents.

The repercussions of extreme ideological adherence can be profound and perilous. Cult members may discover themselves ensnared in a web of psychological and emotional abuse, isolated from their support networks, and ensnared in the clutches of their cult. Yet, the first glimmer of liberation arises with the recognition of the signs of extreme ideological adherence.

Within the pages of "Unveiling the Shadows: Decoding the Signs of Cult Affiliations," we embark on a profound exploration of the labyrinthine world of cults. The book meticulously dissects the distinguishing signs of religious, political, conspiracy theory, spiritual, new age, and celebrity-focused cults. By casting light on the mechanics underpinning extreme ideological adherence, the book seeks to embolden individuals who harbor suspicions of cult involvement. It also beckons true crime enthusiasts with a riveting narrative, offering a profound insight into the psychology and stratagems deployed by these elusive organizations.

In the grand tapestry of understanding, remember: knowledge is power. Armed with an awareness of the signs of extreme ideological adherence, we fortify ourselves and others against the shadows that loom within the realm of cult affiliations.

The Enigma Unveiled: Cults of Personality and the Specter of Authoritarianism

Within the chapters of "Unveiling the Shadows: Decoding the Signs of Cult Affiliations," the enthralling expedition navigates the intriguing realm of cults of personality and authoritarianism. This exploration casts light upon the manifold signs and characteristics intrinsic to cults revolving around charismatic leaders, whether ensconced in the folds of religion, politics, or clandestine conspiracy theories.

For those threading the labyrinth of self-discovery amidst potential cult affiliations or fervent true crime enthusiasts, unraveling the dynamics of these cults promises illumination and empowerment. By deciphering the signs, individuals stand poised to comprehend their own experiences more deeply and to recognize potential hazards looming in the lives of others.

A cardinal sign of a cult of personality lies in the formidable presence of a charismatic leader, one who wields an extraordinary degree of influence over their followers. These leaders, endowed with the power to captivate and sway through charm, eloquence, or the semblance of supernatural prowess, beckon scrutiny into the psychological stratagems employed to manipulate and perpetuate their dominion over devoted disciples.

Furthermore, the exploration extends to diverse categories of cults, ranging from religious and political to conspiracy theory, spiritual, new age, and even the realm of celebrity or fanatical followings. Each category unfurls distinct characteristics and behaviors, a nuanced landscape crucial for recognition.

In the realm of religious cults, we delve into the signs that set them apart from mainstream religions, encompassing isolation from society, rigid dogmas, and the exploitation of followers' vulnerabilities. Political cults, on the contrary, thrive on ideological zeal, groupthink, and the stifling of dissenting voices.

Conspiracy theory cults sprout from the fertile soil of suspicion and mistrust, beckoning those seeking alternative explanations to complex events. Spiritual and new age cults, on their part, exploit the yearning for personal growth and spiritual fulfillment, peddling promises of enlightenment and clandestine wisdom.

Concluding the odyssey, we address the signs characterizing celebrity or fanatical following cults, where the object of veneration is not a religious or political luminary but a celebrity or public figure. These cults unfurl before us, marked by obsessive devotion, blind adulation, and an unwavering willingness to rationalize any actions undertaken by their idol.

By dissecting the myriad manifestations of cults of personality and authoritarianism, readers embark on a journey to discern the red flags and warning signs entwined with these enigmatic groups. This subchapter serves as a beacon, empowering individuals to craft informed decisions, fortify their defenses, and, perhaps, extend a guiding hand to those ensnared within the clutches of these manipulative organizations.

Silencing Echoes: Unraveling the Suppression of Dissent and Critical Thinking in Cult Affiliations

Within the enigmatic realm of cult affiliations, a potent weapon wielded by leaders to fortify their dominion is the suppression of dissent and critical thinking. This subchapter embarks on an odyssey, exposing the subtle signs of this insidious practice across diverse cult types, spanning religious, political, conspiracy theory, spiritual, new age, and celebrity or fanatical followings.

A glaring hallmark of cults lies in their disdain for questioning or challenging the established beliefs and practices. Cult leaders, draped in an aura of infallibility, decree their teachings as absolute truths, erecting an ideological fortress impervious to dissent. Deviation from this sanctioned doctrine invites punitive measures—ranging from isolation and ostracization to physical harm—engendering an environment where critical thinking is stifled, dissent is taboo, and alternative perspectives are shunned.

Another harbinger of suppressed critical thinking is the manipulation of information flow and control over communication channels. Cult leaders assert dominance by meticulously regulating the dissemination of information within the group. Channels are clamped shut, dissenting views expunged, and contradictory evidence swept aside. Through censorship, isolation, or propaganda, leaders curate a narrative that reinforces the cult's ideology, shielding followers from diverse perspectives and cementing control over their thoughts.

Cults, with an artful touch, devalue independent thinking and nurture dependency on the group and its leaders. Mind control tactics, such as thought-stopping phrases, repetitive rituals, and emotional manipulation, mold followers into reliant adherents. By conditioning minds to seek guidance and validation solely from the cult, critical thinking becomes a casualty, and dissent withers in the shadows.

For those ensnared in the labyrinth of potential cult affiliations, recognizing these signs is the first ray of dawn in regaining autonomy and reclaiming the ability to think independently. Understanding the mechanisms behind the suppression of dissent is the compass guiding individuals on the path to liberation.

True crime enthusiasts, delving into the signs of a cult's suppression of dissent, unearth the motivations and behaviors of leaders and followers alike.

It unravels the intricate power dynamics and the psychological machinations that enthrall individuals within these groups.

In conclusion, the suppression of dissent and critical thinking weaves its insidious thread across diverse cult affiliations. Armed with the knowledge to discern these signs and unravel the tactics of cult leaders, individuals emerge fortified against the siren call of these perilous ideologies.

Political Discourse Manipulation: Navigating the Web of Deception

In an age inundated with information, the discerning eye becomes crucial for unraveling the complexities of political discourse manipulation. This subchapter seeks to illuminate the multifaceted ways in which political discourse can be molded, providing keen insights into the signs of cult affiliations within this intricate web.

Manipulation within political discourse often thrives on controlling public opinion to advance a specific agenda. This manipulation encompasses the dissemination of misinformation, propaganda, and the distortion of facts. Recognizing the signs of this manipulation equips individuals with the tools to traverse the political landscape judiciously, guarding against succumbing to cult-like ideologies.

A red flag to heed is the creation of an "us versus them" mentality. Manipulative political discourse habitually segregates people into distinct groups, portraying one as the adversary and the other as virtuous, fabricating a deceptive sense of unity within the cult. This tactic alienates dissenting voices and fortifies groupthink, a hallmark of cult affiliations.

Fear tactics constitute another telltale sign. Manipulative political discourse preys on people's insecurities and anxieties, manipulating emotions to garner support and control. By perpetuating an impending sense of doom or a threat to national security, these cult-like movements cultivate urgency and foster dependence on their leadership.

Language manipulation is a common tool in shaping political discourse within cult affiliations. Political movements associated with cult-like behaviors often employ loaded terms, slogans, and buzzwords to elicit emotional responses and control the narrative. Restricting language confines discourse to a narrow set of terms, effectively manipulating the beliefs and behaviors of followers.

Recognizing signs of cult affiliations within political discourse is indispensable for those ensnared in potential cult groups. This knowledge serves as a potent resource for true crime enthusiasts, unveiling the motivations and tactics employed by cults within the political sphere.

Armed with the ability to critically assess political discourse and identify signs of manipulation, individuals can make informed decisions and engage in constructive, open dialogue. Decoding the signs of cult affiliations within political discourse is pivotal for safeguarding the foundations of a healthy and functioning democracy.

Recruitment Tactics in the Political Cult Landscape

Political cults, weaving ideologies into their fabric, occupy a unique and perilous niche within the realm of cult affiliations. These groups leverage political ideologies to manipulate and control, making comprehension of their recruitment tactics imperative for those suspecting involvement and for true crime enthusiasts seeking to decipher the signs of cult affiliations.

A primary tactic in the arsenal of political cults is the exploitation of social and political unrest. Seizing on the disenchantment or disillusionment of individuals with mainstream politics, these groups offer an alternative community promising to address grievances. Capitalizing on discontent, political cults create a sense of urgency and purpose, luring individuals into their fold.

Charismatic leaders constitute another potent recruitment tool. Armed with the ability to inspire and manipulate, these leaders employ charisma and persuasion to recruit new members. Techniques such as public speaking, personal charm, and promises of a brighter future are wielded to entice vulnerable individuals into the cult's ranks.

Indoctrination and brainwashing emerge as critical tools for controlling followers. Employing mind control, thought reform, and manipulation of information, political cults ensure absolute loyalty and obedience. By regulating information access and manipulating beliefs, these groups solidify their control over individuals.

Group dynamics play a pivotal role in political cult recruitment. Creating a sense of community and belonging, these cults convince followers they are part of an elite group fighting for a common cause. The appeal of belonging and purpose is particularly potent for those feeling isolated from mainstream society.

Fear and intimidation are also prevalent recruitment tactics. Exaggerating external threats or fostering an atmosphere of paranoia keeps followers in a constant state of alertness and dependency.

This fear-based approach ensures unwavering loyalty to the cult and its ideology.

Understanding these recruitment tactics is paramount for identifying and dismantling political cults. Recognizing the signs of a political cult and being informed about their tactics empower individuals to shield themselves and others from falling prey to manipulative strategies.

Five

Signs of a Conspiracy Theory Cult

The Rise of Conspiracy Theories: Unveiling the Shadows

In recent years, the surge in the popularity of conspiracy theories has become a prominent phenomenon, permeating mainstream culture and captivating the minds of individuals who believe they have cult affiliations and true crime enthusiasts alike. A common tactic among these groups is to call out

Cult Leaders and Conspiracy Theories: An Unholy Alliance

One of the distinct signs of a cult is the propagation of conspiracy theories, a manipulation tool exploited by cult leaders to control their followers. In cultivating a distorted worldview where they are the sole purveyors of reliable information, cult leaders create an environment conducive to the flourishing of conspiracy theories. Vulnerable followers, under the influence of cult manipulation, become increasingly receptive to outlandish claims that reinforce their skewed belief system.

Religious cults, often leveraging conspiracy theories to justify their existence and recruit new followers, spread fear and paranoia about external threats. This fear-based manipulation of religious beliefs has, in some instances, led to perilous outcomes, such as mass suicides and acts of violence.

Political cults, too, exploit conspiracy theories to advance their agendas. By promoting narratives that demonize opponents and undermine mainstream institutions, these cults foster an "us versus them" mentality, capitalizing on societal unrest to create a sense of belonging and shared purpose.

Conspiracy theory cults specifically focus on disseminating alternative explanations for historical events, scientific findings, or political developments. In the digital age, these cults thrive in online echo chambers, radicalizing individuals and inciting violence in the pursuit of their beliefs.

In the realm of spirituality, new age cults intertwine esoteric teachings with conspiratorial thinking, creating a narrative where spiritual enlightenment hinges on uncovering hidden truths. However, this quest for secret knowledge often leads to isolation and detachment from reality.

Even in celebrity or fanatical following cults, charismatic figures align themselves with conspiracy theories to enhance their authority and control over devoted followers.

The rise of conspiracy theories within various cult affiliations warrants a critical evaluation of information presented. True crime enthusiasts and those who believe they may be part of a cult must be vigilant, understanding the signs of a cult and the role of conspiracy theories within them to protect themselves from the clutches of dangerous ideologies.

Cult-Like Behaviors Within Conspiracy Groups: Navigating the Shadows

In the labyrinth of conspiracy theories, the distinction between passionate belief and cult-like behaviors becomes crucial. While not all conspiracy groups exhibit cult-like traits, recognizing the signs is imperative. This subchapter aims to unravel the various cult-like behaviors commonly observed within conspiracy groups, shedding light on potential dangers and aiding individuals in identifying cult affiliations.

A pivotal sign of a cult within conspiracy groups is the presence of a charismatic leader wielding significant influence. These leaders, with unwavering convictions and persuasive skills, establish strict hierarchies, demanding unquestioning loyalty from followers.

Manipulation and control are prevalent, leading members to isolation from dissenting voices and fostering dependence on the group. Mind control techniques, such as thought-stopping strategies and information manipulation, further strengthen the leader's hold over followers.

An "us versus them" mentality surfaces, with members considering themselves enlightened while dismissing opposing views as part of a larger conspiracy. This black-and-white thinking often leads to exclusionary practices and hostility towards outsiders.

Coercive practices, such as financial exploitation or forced labor, may be present. Members might be encouraged to donate substantial sums or devote excessive time to the cause, compromising personal well-being.

Recognizing these signs is crucial for those

suspecting cult affiliations. Understanding the dynamics within these groups empowers individuals to protect themselves, seek support, and regain autonomy. Breaking free from the grip of such harmful affiliations requires a cautious approach and professional guidance.

In conclusion, while not all conspiracy groups exhibit cult-like behaviors, awareness of potential signs is essential. Understanding the dynamics of cult-like behavior within these groups allows individuals to navigate involvement cautiously and, if necessary, seek help to break free from harmful affiliations.

Paranoia and Persecution Complex: Unraveling the Shadows

In the intricate web of cult affiliations, paranoia and a persecution complex often intertwine, creating a psychological environment that manipulates and controls followers. This subchapter seeks to explore the intricacies of these tendencies within various types of cults. By deciphering the signs and symptoms associated with paranoia and persecution complex, individuals can gain profound insights into their experiences and potentially liberate themselves from the clutches of cult influence.

Paranoia, characterized by an overwhelming fear of being targeted or harmed by external forces, becomes a potent tool in the hands of cult leaders. Exploiting their followers' vulnerabilities, these leaders amplify the fear, convincing them of constant surveillance or conspiracies against them. This heightened state of paranoia serves a dual purpose—controlling and isolating individuals, making them more dependent on the cult for safety and validation.

Concurrently, a persecution complex, an exaggerated belief in being unfairly targeted, serves as another manipulation tool. Cult leaders foster unquestioning loyalty by convincing followers that they belong to an elite group facing intense opposition. This complex takes root strongly in religious, political, and conspiracy theory cults, where followers perceive themselves as warriors against powerful forces seeking to suppress or annihilate their beliefs.

Identifying signs of paranoia and persecution complex is crucial for those suspecting cult affiliations. Indicators include an incessant feeling of being monitored, irrational fears of persecution, reluctance to trust others, and an inflated sense of importance or uniqueness. Social isolation, encouraged by the cult to discourage contact with perceived threats, is another common outcome.

Recognition of these signs is the initial step towards reclaiming autonomy and breaking free from the grip of cult affiliations. Seeking professional assistance, such as therapy or joining support groups specializing in cult recovery, is instrumental in this process. These experts provide essential guidance, validation, and support in rebuilding one's sense of self and establishing healthy relationships.

Understanding the psychological tactics of cults is pivotal for liberation. By unveiling the shadows of paranoia and persecution complex, individuals can emancipate themselves and forge a path towards a life free from the influence of destructive cults.

Confirmation Bias and Information Control: Decoding the Manipulation

In the intricate landscape of cults and extreme belief systems, confirmation bias and information control emerge as powerful tools shaping the minds of their followers. A nuanced understanding of these concepts is indispensable for individuals suspecting cult affiliations or for true crime enthusiasts aiming to decode the subtle signs of cult involvement. This subchapter delves into the perilous interplay between confirmation bias and information control, unveiling the tactics employed by cults across various domains.

Confirmation bias, a natural human inclination to seek information validating existing beliefs, becomes a potent weapon in the hands of cults. Leaders carefully curate information, ensuring that only a narrow range of ideas and perspectives aligning with their ideology are presented. This deliberate control creates an echo chamber effect, reinforcing existing beliefs and rendering followers resistant to alternative viewpoints.

Information control, a formidable tool in the cult arsenal, serves to maintain influence and dominance. Through censorship, isolation, and manipulation, cults restrict access to outside information. Dissenting opinions are actively discouraged or punished, fostering dependency on the cult for information. This isolation hinders critical thinking, indoctrinating individuals into the cult's belief system.

These manipulative tactics are prevalent across various niches, including religious, political, conspiracy theory, spiritual, new age, and celebrity or fanatical followings. Regardless of the niche, confirmation bias and information control are pervasive, aimed at manipulating and controlling cult members. Recognizing these signs is vital for those suspecting cult involvement or for true crime enthusiasts aiming to understand the consequences of these manipulative tactics.

By shedding light on confirmation bias and information control within cults, this subchapter aims to empower readers to recognize these insidious tactics. Through education and awareness, individuals can shield themselves from falling victim to cult manipulation. True crime enthusiasts gain insights into the world of extreme belief systems, decoding the signs of cult affiliations and understanding the perilous consequences of these subtle manipulations.

The Role of Social Media in Cult-like Conspiracy Communities: Navigating the Digital Abyss

In our digital age, the rise of social media has brought about a paradigm shift in the way communities form and ideologies spread. Among these digital spaces are communities with cult-like tendencies, especially those entrenched in conspiracy theories. While social media serves as a platform for connectivity and information sharing, it inadvertently fosters the growth of such communities, potentially drawing individuals into cult-like affiliations.

The unrestricted access to information on social media is a double-edged sword. While it allows users to explore diverse perspectives, it also facilitates the creation of echo chambers. Users can easily find communities that align with their existing beliefs, fostering an environment where alternative viewpoints are suppressed. This echo chamber effect isolates individuals, strengthening their affiliation with the cult-like community.

Algorithmic reinforcement on social media platforms contributes to the entrenchment of users in conspiracy communities. Platforms aim to maximize user engagement by showing content that aligns with their existing beliefs, creating a self-reinforcing cycle. As users engage more with content, they unwittingly contribute to the spread of misinformation, amplifying the influence of cult-like ideologies.

Social media also plays a pivotal role in the emergence of virtual cult leaders. Traditional cults rely on charismatic leaders to manipulate and control followers. In the digital realm, individuals can attain cult-like status by amassing a large following and disseminating their ideologies through social media. These virtual cult leaders exploit their influence to control followers' beliefs and actions.

For individuals who believe they have cult affiliations or true crime enthusiasts, recognizing the signs of a cult-like conspiracy community is vital. While social media can be a gateway to these communities, critical discernment is necessary when consuming information online. Awareness of the signs of a cult, whether religious, political, spiritual, or conspiracy-based, is crucial for protecting oneself from potential harm.

In "Unveiling the Shadows: Decoding the Signs of Cult Affiliations," we delve into the intricate dynamics of cult-like conspiracy communities and the role social media plays in their growth.

By understanding these dynamics, individuals can navigate the digital landscape responsibly and shield themselves from falling victim to harmful ideologies.

Escalation into Violence and Extremism: Unmasking the Dark Path

Within the enigmatic realm of cults, where charismatic leaders weave intricate ideologies, there exists a perilous trajectory that leads some down a path of darkness. This subchapter, "Escalation into Violence and Extremism," unveils the warning signs and red flags indicating a cult's descent into an alarming abyss.

For those suspecting cult affiliations and true crime enthusiasts, this subchapter serves as an essential guide, elucidating the transition from seemingly innocuous beliefs to extremist actions. It explores various cult niches, including religious, political, conspiracy theory, spiritual, new age, and celebrity or fanatical following cults, deciphering the signs of escalation into violence and extremism.

While signs of a cult often involve manipulation, isolation, and control, the stakes elevate significantly when violence and extremism become part of the equation. In religious cults, this escalation may manifest through radical interpretations of scriptures, rituals involving self-harm or sacrifice, or the propagation of apocalyptic ideologies. Political cults may resort to terrorism, assassinations, or inciting rebellion to further their agenda.

Conspiracy theory cults, fueled by paranoia and mistrust, easily cross into violence and extremism. This may involve drastic measures against perceived enemies, cyberattacks, or planning acts of domestic terrorism. Spiritual and new age cults, promising enlightenment, may unexpectedly evolve into dangerous organizations, coercing members into engaging in abusive rituals or committing violent acts.

Lastly, celebrity or fanatical following cults may escalate into violence as fanatical devotion leads to the suppression of critical thinking. Followers may engage in violent acts to protect their idol or emulate their beliefs.

Understanding signs of escalation into violence and extremism is crucial for those suspecting cult affiliations. By recognizing these warning signs, individuals can seek help and escape before it's too late. For true crime enthusiasts, this subchapter offers insights into the dark underbelly of cults and their potential for violence, providing a unique perspective on criminal behavior rooted in extreme beliefs.

In "Unveiling the Shadows: Decoding the Signs of Cult Affiliations," this subchapter serves as a crucial resource, shedding light on the treacherous path that some cults embark upon, empowering readers to recognize the signs of escalation into violence and extremism within various cult niches.

Six

Signs of a Spiritual Cult

Spiritualism vs. Cultism: Navigating the Delicate Boundary

In our contemporary world, marked by an incessant quest for meaning and connection, the demarcation between spiritualism and cultism can often become obscured. It is imperative to discern between these divergent paths, as the consequences of inadvertently descending into a cult can be profoundly damaging. In this subchapter, we embark on an exploration of the nuanced distinctions between spiritualism and cultism, shedding light on discernible signs to aid individuals in navigating these realms with sagacity.

Spiritualism, at its essence, constitutes a profoundly personal and introspective expedition. It involves delving into one's inner self, forging a connection with a higher power, and embarking on the pursuit of enlightenment. Practices such as meditation, prayer, and rituals form the tapestry of spiritualism, all centered around personal growth and connection to a larger universal truth. An inherent aspect of spiritualism is the encouragement for individuals to chart their own course, fostering an environment that reveres the diversity of perspectives within the spiritual community.

Conversely, cultism thrives on manipulation, control, and the exploitation of vulnerable individuals. Cults often showcase charismatic leaders adept at employing coercive tactics to amass power and authority over their followers. Employing mind control techniques, cults isolate individuals from their families and friends, instilling a pervasive sense of fear, dependence, and unwavering loyalty.

Blind obedience is a cornerstone of cult dynamics, stifling individuality and critical thinking.

To assist individuals in identifying the signs of cult affiliations, it is imperative to discern the key characteristics of cults across various contexts, be it religious, political, conspiracy theory, new age, or celebrity/fanatical followings. There exist common red flags that warrant attention:

1. Absolute control over members' lives and decisions.

2. Isolation from friends and family outside the cult.

3. Manipulative tactics to exploit and extract resources from followers.

4. A charismatic leader who demands unquestioning loyalty.

5. Suppression of critical thinking and independent beliefs.

6. The presence of harmful practices or abuse within the group.

7. A sense of superiority and exclusivity, often accompanied by disdain for outsiders.

Understanding these signs equips individuals with the acumen to better shield themselves from inadvertently affiliating with harmful groups. The ability to discern the difference between spiritualism and cultism is paramount for maintaining personal autonomy and overall well-being.

In the upcoming work, "Unveiling the Shadows: Decoding the Signs of Cult Affiliations," our goal is to empower individuals who suspect they may have cult affiliations. This book serves as a valuable resource for true crime enthusiasts, providing profound insights into the psychology and mechanisms underpinning cult operations. By illuminating the signs across various cult types, we aspire to furnish readers with the knowledge and tools indispensable for navigating these intricate waters and reclaiming their freedom.

Exploitation of Spiritual Seekers: Illuminating the Shadows

Within the realm of cult affiliations, a particularly poignant facet that demands heightened scrutiny is the exploitation of spiritual seekers. Across history, instances abound where individuals earnestly seeking answers, enlightenment, or connection with a higher existence have fallen prey to the machinations of charismatic leaders and manipulative organizations. This subchapter meticulously unravels the signs and dynamics of such exploitation, casting a revealing light on the dark underbelly of spiritual cults.

Spiritual seekers are often propelled by an authentic desire for inner growth and transcendence. Their quest may encompass the pursuit of meaning, purpose, or a profound connection to a higher power. Regrettably, unscrupulous individuals adept at recognizing vulnerabilities exploit these yearnings. They present themselves as enlightened beings possessing exclusive access to secret knowledge or divine wisdom. These charismatic leaders deftly manipulate the aspirations of spiritual seekers, ensnaring them within the intricate web of their influence.

A glaring sign of a spiritual cult lies in the

leader's inflated ego and grandiose claims. Portraying themselves as the ultimate authority on spirituality, these leaders assert possession of unique insights or divine messages. They foster a power dynamic wherein followers are conditioned to revere and unquestioningly obey them. This dynamic effectively curtails individual growth and cultivates dependency, ensnaring seekers within the clutches of the cult.

Exploitation manifests in various forms, including financial manipulation. Cult leaders frequently demand exorbitant donations or fees for access to their teachings or services, promising spiritual enlightenment or material abundance in return. This preys on the desires and vulnerabilities of followers, leading to potential isolation, financial ruin, and emotional distress.

Moreover, spiritual cults may resort to coercive tactics to assert control. These tactics encompass isolation from friends and family, sleep deprivation, and forced labor. By severing seekers from their support systems and subjecting them to intense physical and emotional stress, cult leaders gain absolute control over their lives.

For those who suspect they may be involved in a spiritual cult, recognizing the signs of exploitation is imperative. It necessitates questioning leaders who claim exclusive access to truth, advocate blind obedience, or demand excessive financial contributions. Seeking support from trusted friends, family, or professionals specializing in cult recovery becomes paramount in breaking free from the clutches of exploitation.

"Unveiling the Shadows: Decoding the Signs of Cult Affiliations" aspires to empower individuals to recognize warning signs and extricate themselves from abusive cult environments. By shedding light on the exploitation of spiritual seekers, this subchapter aims to shield vulnerable individuals from falling prey to the manipulation and control wielded by charismatic cult leaders.

Manipulation of Beliefs and Practices: Unraveling the Threads of Control

Within the intricate web of cult affiliations, the manipulation of beliefs and practices emerges as one of the most potent tools wielded by these groups. Whether rooted in religious doctrines, political ideologies, conspiracy theories, spirituality, new age philosophies, or the allure of celebrity, cults share a common objective: the dominion over the minds and actions of their members. This sub-chapter aims to dissect the signs and techniques employed in this manipulation, a critical understanding for those suspecting cult involvement and true crime enthusiasts seeking to fathom the mysteries surrounding these enigmatic groups.

At the heart of cult dynamics lies belief manipulation. These organizations strategically intertwine psychological and emotional tactics to indoctrinate and control their members. Exploiting vulnerabilities, they promise answers, purpose, and a sense of belonging, crafting profound belief systems that purport to offer an all-encompassing solution to life's existential questions. By preying on fears, insecurities, and the fundamental human need for connection, cult leaders establish a formidable influence over their followers.

The practices embedded within cults are meticulously designed to fortify the beliefs instilled in their members. Rituals, ceremonies, and group activities are carefully crafted to deepen the sense of community and allegiance. These practices often involve sensory manipulation, employing techniques such as chanting, repetitive actions, or inducing intense emotional experiences that can lead to altered states of consciousness. By exerting control over the environment and regulating personal habits, cults reinforce their authority and foster an atmosphere of dependency.

Recognition of the signs of belief and practice manipulation is paramount for individuals concerned about their involvement in a cult. Red flags include excessive control over personal decisions, isolation from friends and family, strict adherence to rituals, and a pervasive sense of fear or guilt for questioning the group's teachings. True crime enthusiasts can study these signs to comprehend the intricate dynamics behind cult operations and the profound repercussions they exert on individuals and society.

"Unveiling the Shadows: Decoding the Signs of Cult Affiliations" delves deep into the manipulation of beliefs and practices across various cult types. By scrutinizing the signs of religious, political, conspiracy theory-based, spiritual, new age, and celebrity cults, this book unveils the techniques employed to control and exploit vulnerable individuals. Offering insights and practical advice, it furnishes a roadmap for those seeking to extricate themselves from the clutches of these manipulative groups.

Cult Leaders as Gurus or Spiritual Authorities: The Charismatic Puppeteers

In the labyrinthine world of cult affiliations, a recurring theme that transcends various cult types is the presence of charismatic leaders who cast themselves as gurus or spiritual authorities.

Possessing a magnetic personality and an artful knack for manipulation, these individuals attract and control followers within their respective cults.

Gurus within religious cults tap into the innate human desire for spiritual enlightenment, positioning themselves as the ultimate repositories of divine knowledge. They claim exclusive insights into the nature of the universe, promising salvation or a heightened state of consciousness to their followers. Through meticulously crafted teachings, they instill a dependency on their leadership, gradually eroding critical thinking and fostering unwavering loyalty.

Political cults, in contrast, exploit the fervor and dedication of their followers towards a specific political ideology or figure. The charismatic leader presents themselves as the embodiment of the ideology, providing followers with a sense of purpose and direction. Leveraging fear-mongering tactics, they cultivate a cult-like atmosphere that discourages dissent and demands unswerving loyalty.

Conspiracy theory cults often revolve around charismatic figures who claim possession of secret knowledge and insights into hidden truths. Exploiting the natural curiosity of individuals seeking answers to complex questions, these leaders position themselves as the sole reliable source of information. They manipulate followers by fostering an "us versus them" mentality, demonizing those who question their beliefs and fostering a sense of persecution.

Leaders within spiritual and new age cults appeal to followers in search of deeper meaning and connection. Casting themselves as enlightened beings capable of guiding followers toward spiritual awakening, these leaders employ esoteric practices and rituals to create a sense of exclusivity and mystery, solidifying their authority.

Celebrity or fanatical following cults coalesce around charismatic public figures with substantial followings. These leaders exploit their followers' adoration and fascination, manipulating emotions and fostering dependency. They often use their influence to encourage extreme behaviors and maintain control over their followers.

Recognition of the signs of cult affiliation is crucial for individuals who suspect their involvement in such a group. Understanding the role of charismatic leaders as gurus or spiritual authorities constitutes a fundamental aspect of this process. By illuminating the tactics employed by these leaders across various cult types, individuals can begin to reclaim their autonomy and shield themselves from further manipulation.

In "Unveiling the Shadows: Decoding the Signs of Cult Affiliations," we delve deeper into the intricate dynamics between cult leaders and their followers. Through comprehensive analysis and real-life case studies, we provide valuable insights for people who believe they have cult affiliations, as well as true crime enthusiasts. Our book caters to a wide range of niches, including signs of a cult, signs of a religious cult, signs of a political cult, signs of a conspiracy theory cult, signs of a spiritual cult, signs of a new age cult, and signs of a celebrity or fanatical following cult. By arming yourself with knowledge and awareness, you can break free from the clutches of cult affiliations and regain control of your life.

Indoctrination and Thought Reform: Deciphering the Machinations of Cults

Within the complex landscape of cult affiliations, the ominous forces of indoctrination and thought reform emerge as pivotal players in shaping individuals' beliefs, behaviors, and identities. This subchapter embarks on an exploration of the insidious methods utilized by a spectrum of cults, ranging from religious and political to conspiracy theory, spiritual, new age, and those centered around celebrity or fanatical followings. By unraveling these mechanisms, readers, whether suspecting cult affiliations or true crime enthusiasts, can glean profound insights into the inner workings of these enigmatic groups.

1. Understanding Indoctrination:
Indoctrination, a systematic process that subtly

influences individuals to adopt specific beliefs or ideologies without critical examination, serves as the linchpin for many cults. This section delves deep into the mechanics of indoctrination, shedding light on its nuanced components such as isolation, information control, and the manipulation of emotions.

2. Thought Reform Techniques:

Thought reform, synonymous with brainwashing, constitutes a coercive process aimed at restructuring an individual's thoughts, attitudes, and behaviors to align with the cult's doctrine. This section ventures into the realm of common thought reform techniques employed by cults. From love-bombing to fear-based control, guilt induction, and the influence of charismatic leaders, the intricacies of these manipulative tactics are unveiled.

3. Signs of a Cult:

This section undertakes a comprehensive examination of the distinct signs indicating cult affiliations across diverse niches. It scrutinizes the unmistakable markers of religious cults, political cults, conspiracy theory cults, spiritual cults, new age cults, and celebrity/fanatical following cults.

Armed with this knowledge, readers can adeptly identify potential harm and safeguard themselves or those close to them.

4. Breaking Free: Recovery and Support:

Liberating oneself from a cult's clutches is a formidable and emotionally taxing journey. This section extends a guiding hand, offering insights on seeking support, reconstructing one's identity, and navigating the recovery process. A repository of resources, including support groups, cult recovery therapists, and pertinent literature, equips individuals with the tools needed to reclaim their lives.

Indoctrination and thought reform techniques wielded by cults are formidable tools, manipulating individuals into a state of unquestioning obedience. Recognizing the signs of cult affiliations across diverse niches empowers individuals to shield themselves and others from falling victim to these groups. By deciphering the tactics employed by cults, individuals can regain autonomy, break free from harmful influences, and embark on a journey of healing and self-discovery.

Cultic Practices in New Age Movements: Navigating the Labyrinth of Spirituality

In the expansive realm of human spirituality, where seekers pursue enlightenment, healing, and personal growth, New Age movements have emerged as a significant phenomenon. While many practitioners genuinely seek truth and transformation, it is imperative to be vigilant regarding potential cultic practices within these movements.

New Age movements, characterized by a fusion of beliefs and practices from diverse spiritual, religious, and metaphysical traditions, typically emphasize inner harmony, self-realization, and the development of psychic abilities. However, within this vast tapestry, signs may emerge that hint at the presence of cultic practices.

A distinctive red flag within New Age movements is the presence of a charismatic leader claiming exclusive knowledge or special powers. These leaders often wield significant control, manipulating beliefs, behaviors, and personal relationships while discouraging critical thinking and fostering unquestioning devotion.

Isolation of followers from mainstream society represents another ominous sign. Cultic New Age groups may advocate cutting ties with family and friends who do not share their beliefs, creating an insular community that reinforces its own ideologies. This isolation facilitates leaders in exerting control and manipulating followers more effectively.

Financial exploitation is a prevalent characteristic of cultic practices within New Age movements. Leaders may coerce members into donating substantial sums, promising spiritual blessings or advancement in return. These financial demands can lead to the impoverishment of followers, fostering a sense of dependency on the group and its leader.

Manipulative techniques such as mind control, thought-stopping, and the suppression of dissenting opinions are frequently employed by cultic New Age movements. These practices are designed to maintain obedience and submissiveness, preventing followers from questioning or challenging the group's beliefs and actions.

Individuals suspecting cult affiliations or true crime enthusiasts must be vigilant regarding signs of a cult within New Age movements. Recognizing these signs is crucial for safeguarding against potential exploitation, manipulation, and harm.

In conclusion, while not all New Age movements exhibit cultic practices, it is essential to remain vigilant and aware of potential signs. Understanding the indicators of a cult within the context of New Age movements empowers individuals to protect themselves from exploitation and manipulation, fostering a safer and more informed spiritual exploration.

Seven

Signs of a New Age Cult

The Magnetic Allure of Unconventional Spiritual Practices

The surge in popularity of New Age movements is a testament to the growing fascination with alternative paths to enlightenment and self-discovery. As we delve deeper into the allure of these movements, it becomes evident that their appeal is multifaceted, catering to the diverse needs of individuals from various walks of life.

At the heart of the attraction lies the universal human desire for personal growth and self-improvement. New Age movements present an array of transformative practices, such as meditation, energy healing, and holistic therapies, promising a journey towards enhanced well-being and spiritual awakening. For those who believe they have cult affiliations, these practices offer not only a roadmap to self-discovery but also a sanctuary for introspection and personal development.

Beyond individual growth, the sense of community fostered by New Age movements is a powerful magnet. In a world where many feel isolated or disconnected, these movements provide a refuge where like-minded individuals can come together. True crime enthusiasts, often drawn to unconventional communities, find solace in the non-judgmental atmosphere created by New Age movements. This communal aspect not only fosters a sense of belonging but also serves as a support system for those navigating their unique spiritual journeys.

The inclusivity and flexibility of New Age movements contribute significantly to their appeal.

Unlike traditional religious or political cults, these movements embrace a wide spectrum of beliefs and practices. This open-minded approach allows individuals to explore diverse spiritual paths, accommodating everything from signs of a religious cult to signs of a conspiracy theory cult. New Age movements become a melting pot of ideologies, providing a platform for seekers to find resonance with their personal truths.

Moreover, New Age movements challenge societal norms and offer alternative perspectives on life, resonating with those disillusioned with mainstream ideologies. By encouraging followers to question established systems and beliefs, these movements empower individuals to forge their unique paths. The unconventional ideas and practices embraced by New Age movements become a source of empowerment and liberation for those seeking to break free from the confines of conventional thinking.

While the appeal of New Age movements is undeniable, a cautious approach is crucial. As with any phenomenon, there are potential pitfalls, hidden dangers, and manipulative tactics that warrant scrutiny. Individuals are urged to remain vigilant, be aware of the signs of a cult, and maintain a balanced perspective when engaging with New Age practices.

In conclusion, the allure of New Age movements lies in their promise of personal growth, community, inclusivity, and alternative perspectives. These movements attract a diverse range of individuals, including those who believe they have cult affiliations and true crime enthusiasts, by offering a unique blend of transformative practices and a sense of belonging. However, it is imperative to approach these movements with discernment and critical thinking to ensure a safe and enriching exploration of one's spiritual journey.

Cult-Like Hierarchies and Power Structures: A Detailed Exploration

In the intricate tapestry of cult affiliations, perhaps one of the most distinctive features is the presence of cult-like hierarchies and power structures. These systems, meticulously crafted, serve as the backbone of control, manipulating followers and securing their unwavering devotion. This subchapter will navigate the nuanced workings of such hierarchies, shedding light on their commonalities and the varied manifestations across different cult affiliations.

Irrespective of whether a cult is rooted in religion, politics, conspiracy theories, spirituality, the New Age movement, or centered around a celebrity or fanatical following, certain red flags can be discerned to identify the existence of a cult-like hierarchy. A pivotal sign lies in the charismatic leader who assumes absolute authority, revered as an infallible figure. These leaders, exploiting the vulnerabilities of their followers, employ manipulative tactics to assert control over their thoughts, beliefs, and actions.

The hierarchical structure within cults is typically rigid, with the leader positioned at the apex, followed by a select inner circle entrusted with enforcing the leader's will. This inner circle enjoys special privileges and acts as the guardian of the cult's control over its members. Dissent and independent thought find little room within these power structures, emphasizing conformity and loyalty.

Cult-like hierarchies further employ strategies to isolate members from the external world, both physically and psychologically. Physical isolation might involve discouraging or outright prohibiting interactions with non-cult individuals. Psychological isolation employs techniques such as information control, thought reform, and groupthink to ensure a homogeneous mindset within the group.

For individuals suspecting their involvement in a cult or for true crime enthusiasts seeking to decipher the dynamics behind cult affiliations, understanding the signs of a cult-like hierarchy is paramount. Recognition of these characteristics offers insight into the psychological mechanisms at play, potentially aiding individuals in extricating themselves or others from the clutches of such power structures.

As we delve into subsequent chapters, the exploration of cult affiliations across diverse niches, including religious, political, conspiracy theory-based, spiritual, New Age, and celebrity or fanatical following cults, will provide readers with a comprehensive understanding of the distinctive markers associated with each. Armed with this knowledge, individuals can better recognize and navigate the intricacies of cult-like hierarchies and power structures.

The Pervasive Influence of Materialism and Consumerism in Cult Affiliations

In unraveling the complexities of cult affiliations, a crucial aspect to explore is the role played by materialism and consumerism in the genesis and perpetuation of these groups. Materialism, an obsessive focus on acquiring material possessions, and consumerism, the belief that happiness stems from the consumption of products and services, significantly contribute to the manipulation and control wielded by cult leaders.

A telltale sign of a cult is the exploitation of individuals' aspirations for material wealth and success. Cult leaders entice followers with promises of a life filled with abundance, including material possessions, financial prosperity, and elevated social status. This allure establishes a potent hold over followers who become convinced that their salvation lies in adhering to the leader's teachings.

Materialism and consumerism within cults serve as tools of control. Cult leaders may restrict access to material possessions and resources, fostering a dependency on the group for basic needs. By manipulating and controlling the material possessions of their followers, leaders ensure a tight grip, making it challenging for individuals to extricate themselves from the cult.

Consumerism also plays a pivotal role in the formation of cult-like followings. In the contemporary world, individuals often seek meaning and purpose, and cults exploit this existential longing. By presenting themselves as the answer to their followers' quest for fulfillment, cult leaders create a sense of belonging and purpose. They convince followers that their materialistic desires can be satisfied by adhering to the group's teachings, perpetuating a cycle of consumption and dependency.

Understanding the role of materialism and consumerism in cult affiliations is essential for those suspecting their involvement in such groups. Recognizing the manipulation tactics employed by cult leaders, such as the promise of material wealth or control over possessions, can empower individuals to break free from the clutches of these organizations.

For true crime enthusiasts, delving into materialism and consumerism within cult affiliations offers valuable insights into the psychology and tactics of cult leaders. It sheds light on the vulnerabilities they exploit and the mechanisms used to maintain control over followers.

By decoding the signs of materialism and consumerism within cult affiliations, individuals arm themselves with knowledge and awareness, enabling them to identify and protect themselves from the influence of cults. This understanding acts as a shield against manipulation and control, fostering autonomy and well-being.

Escaping the Allure of a New Age Cult: A Journey to Liberation

Within the intricate landscape of cult affiliations, New Age cults emerge as particularly beguiling and deceptive entities. Masked by the façade of peaceful, enlightened communities focused on personal growth and spiritual awakening, these groups harbor a dark underbelly of manipulation, control, and psychological exploitation. If suspicions arise regarding involvement in a New Age cult, recognizing the signs becomes paramount, initiating a journey to escape its clutches.

A distinctive hallmark of New Age cults is the charismatic leader professing exclusive knowledge or spiritual enlightenment. This leader, often employing charm and persuasive abilities, attracts vulnerable individuals seeking answers and a sense of belonging. While promising personal transformation and spiritual enlightenment, these leaders are adept manipulators, exploiting followers for personal gain.

Another red flag indicative of a New Age cult is the employment of isolation and control tactics. Members are encouraged to sever ties with family and friends critical of the group's beliefs. This deliberate isolation serves to control and limit the influence of external perspectives, facilitating the cult's stronghold on the minds of its members.

Financial exploitation is a prevalent aspect within New Age cults. Members are often required to donate substantial sums of money or assets to the group, ostensibly to support its mission or attain spiritual advancement. This financial dependence deepens the psychological hold the cult has on its followers, making it challenging for individuals to break free.

Escaping the clutches of a New Age cult necessitates courage and a robust support system. Reaching out to trusted friends or family members capable of providing emotional and practical support becomes crucial throughout the process. Educating oneself about cult dynamics and manipulation tactics proves empowering, aiding in the recognition and resistance of these techniques.

Seeking professional assistance from therapists or support groups specializing in cult recovery is highly recommended. These professionals guide individuals through the healing process, assisting in rebuilding a sense of self and regaining control over life.

The journey to extricate oneself from a New Age cult is undeniably challenging, yet it is feasible. By recognizing the signs, seeking support, and prioritizing well-being, individuals can escape the clutches of a New Age cult and reclaim their freedom and individuality. This journey towards liberation entails self-discovery, resilience, and the unwavering commitment to break free from the psychological chains that bind.

Signs of a Celebrity or Fanatical Following Cult

The Allure of Celebrity Culture: A Deeper Exploration

In the ever-evolving landscape of contemporary society, the allure of celebrity culture stands as an undeniable force. We find ourselves in an era where the lives of the rich and famous are laid bare for public consumption, their every move scrutinized and dissected. Yet, the question persists: What is it about these celebrities that captivates us so profoundly? And how does our societal obsession with fame and fortune intersect with the signs of cult affiliations?

Celebrities, with their glamorous lifestyles and seemingly flawless existence, have seamlessly transitioned into modern-day idols for a multitude of people. This idolization often borders on obsession, as individuals immerse themselves in the images and narratives projected by these icons. From magazine covers to billboards and social media feeds, the ubiquity of celebrity presence fosters a sense of familiarity and connection that can be intoxicating. Many individuals look up to these figures as role models, aspiring to emulate their success and lifestyle.

However, this elevation of celebrities to quasi-deity status can lead to perilous territory—the formation of cult-like followings. In the vast realm of cult affiliations, celebrity fandoms exhibit signs reminiscent of cult dynamics. The intense devotion and loyalty toward a particular celebrity can foster a sense of community and belonging, akin to that found in religious or political cults. Fans may adopt the beliefs and values of their idol, blindly following their every word and action.

A pervasive sign of a celebrity cult lies in the erosion of critical thinking. Fans, overwhelmed by their adoration, may find themselves unable to acknowledge any faults or flaws in their idol. This blind devotion creates a protective bubble around the celebrity, preventing fans from questioning or evaluating their actions and behaviors. The echo chamber of unwavering support can become a breeding ground for dangerous distortions.

Moreover, the allure of celebrity culture extends into the realms of conspiracy theories and new age spirituality. Certain celebrities actively promote and endorse these fringe beliefs, accumulating a following of individuals who subscribe to these alternative theories and practices. This convergence of celebrity status and unconventional beliefs can give rise to the formation of cult-like groups, where fans adopt these beliefs as absolute truths.

For those grappling with the suspicion of cult

affiliations, it is paramount to recognize and evaluate the signs of a celebrity or fanatical following cult. This subchapter aims to delve into the distinct signs associated with celebrity cults and illuminate their intersections with other forms of cult affiliations. By comprehending the allure of celebrity culture and its potential dangers, individuals can embark on a journey to unravel the shadows of their own beliefs and affiliations.

The Dynamics of Celebrity Cults: Unveiling the Complex Tapestry

In the complex fabric of contemporary society, the allure of celebrities has woven a narrative of intense admiration and emotional connection that transcends mere fandom. Yet, this admiration, in certain instances, morphs into something more insidious—a celebrity cult. This subchapter delves into the intricate dynamics of these cults, unraveling the signs that may indicate their existence.

Celebrity cults, a unique amalgamation of traditional cult dynamics and fervent fandom, revolve around a charismatic celebrity figure who wields substantial influence over their followers. The dynamics of these cults blur the lines between adoration and manipulation, creating a complex web of interactions.

A pivotal characteristic of celebrity cults is the presence of a powerful leader figure who becomes the focal point of worship. This individual may possess exceptional talent, charisma, or beauty, drawing people in and holding their attention. Followers often elevate the celebrity to an almost divine status, believing that they hold the key to enlightenment or salvation.

Exclusive community creation is another dynamic within celebrity cults. Followers form a tight-knit group, isolating themselves from those who do not share the same fervor. This sense of belonging and acceptance within the community strengthens the bonds between members while simultaneously cutting them off from external influences.

In some instances, celebrity cults adopt traits reminiscent of religious or political cults. The leader may advocate specific beliefs or ideologies, urging followers to adopt them unquestioningly. This blind devotion can lead to a distortion of reality, as critical thinking is supplanted by loyalty to the celebrity's words or actions.

The advent of social media has catalyzed the growth of celebrity cults, providing an ideal environment for these communities to flourish. Online platforms facilitate fan connections, allowing them to easily reinforce each other's beliefs. The constant exposure to curated images and narratives further solidifies the idolization of the celebrity figure, creating a formidable challenge for followers attempting to break free from the cult's grasp.

Recognizing the signs of a celebrity cult is imperative for those suspecting cult affiliations or for true crime enthusiasts studying this intriguing subject. By understanding the dynamics at play, individuals gain insight into their own experiences or can extend help to those ensnared within these cults.

In the chapters to come, we will explore the signs of various cults, spanning religious, political, conspiracy theory, spiritual, new age, and celebrity or fanatical following cults. Through a comprehensive analysis, we aim to illuminate the dark corners of cult affiliations, providing guidance for those seeking liberation from their clutches.

Obsession and Idolization of Celebrities: Navigating the Complex Terrain

In the ever-evolving landscape of today's media-driven society, the obsession and idolization of celebrities have reached unprecedented levels, shaping the way individuals perceive and interact with public figures. From Hollywood stars to musicians, athletes, and social media influencers, the magnetic allure of these celebrities often blurs the line between admiration and an unhealthy, cult-like following. This subchapter delves into the multifaceted signs and implications of the widespread obsession and idolization of celebrities, aiming to shed light on the potential dangers it poses to individuals and society as a whole.

Celebrities, with their glamorous lifestyles and seemingly perfect images, possess the influential power to captivate and sway the hearts of millions. This allure frequently transforms into a fanatical following, where individuals may exhibit signs reminiscent of cult-like behavior. Whether it's a religious, political, conspiratorial, spiritual, or even a new age cult, the underlying signs manifest striking similarities across diverse cult affiliations.

A conspicuous sign of an unhealthy celebrity obsession is the unquestioning loyalty exhibited by individuals toward their idol. This blind allegiance, often fueled by an intense emotional connection, can be manipulated by charismatic celebrities seeking to maintain and extend their influence over their followers.

Another red flag is the isolation of individuals

from their social circles, including friends, family, and even their own core values and beliefs. A cult-like following may demand complete devotion to the celebrity, leading individuals to sever ties with loved ones who question their infatuation. This isolation further strengthens the bond between the idol and their followers, creating a perilous echo chamber that reinforces extreme behaviors.

Moreover, the idolization of celebrities can result in a loss of personal identity, where individuals define themselves solely through their connection to the celebrity. This may involve adopting the values, mannerisms, and even physical appearance of the idol, leading to a profound disconnection from one's true self. This loss of self can have profound consequences on an individual's mental and emotional well-being.

For those suspecting they may be ensnared in the web of a celebrity or fanatical following cult, seeking support and guidance is imperative. Recognizing the signs of cult affiliations serves as the initial step toward breaking free from the grip of obsession and rediscovering one's personal identity. "Unveiling the Shadows" provides valuable insights and practical tools to help individuals navigate these intricate dynamics and regain control over their lives.

In the broader societal context, it becomes imperative that we remain vigilant and educate ourselves about the potential dangers of celebrity idolization. By understanding the signs and implications of cult-like behavior, we can collectively protect ourselves and our loved ones from falling victim to unhealthy obsessions and reclaim our autonomy in the face of media-driven influences.

Manipulation and Exploitation by Celebrity Leaders: Unmasking the Dark Influence

In the complex realm of cult affiliations, one of the most intriguing yet concerning aspects involves the entanglement of celebrity leaders. These charismatic figures, often revered by their followers, wield an uncanny ability to manipulate and exploit their fanatical followings. "Unveiling the Shadows: Decoding the Signs of Cult Affiliations" delves deep into the world of celebrity-led cults, exposing the dark side of their influence.

Celebrities, with their talent, beauty, or charisma, have perennially held an allure for the masses. However, when these individuals exploit their fame to establish cult-like followings, the consequences can be dire. This subchapter aims to explore the signs and red flags associated with the manipulation and exploitation tactics employed by these celebrity leaders.

A key indicator of a celebrity-led cult is the excessive adoration and idolization of the leader. These individuals often possess a magnetic personality that attracts vulnerable individuals seeking guidance and purpose. Through carefully crafted personas, they create an image of infallibility, making it nearly impossible for their followers to question their actions or motives.

Another hallmark of these cults is the isolation

and control exerted over their followers. Celebrity leaders may employ tactics such as limiting contact with the outside world, encouraging dependence on the group, or using fear and guilt to maintain control. By isolating their followers, they can further manipulate their beliefs and actions, creating a sense of dependency on the leader and the cult.

Financial exploitation is another prevalent aspect of celebrity-led cults. These leaders often encourage their followers to make significant financial contributions or even surrender their assets in the name of the cult's mission or cause. Through guilt, manipulation, or promises of spiritual enlightenment, they exploit their followers' trust and generosity, enriching themselves at their expense.

"Unveiling the Shadows" also delves into the psychological manipulation techniques employed by these celebrity leaders. From gaslighting and coercive persuasion to thought reform and mind control, these tactics are used to strip followers of their autonomy and critical thinking abilities, further perpetuating the leader's control over their lives.

By decoding the signs of manipulation and exploitation by celebrity leaders, this subchapter aims to empower individuals who may suspect their involvement in a cult to recognize the warning signs. It serves as a resource for true crime enthusiasts and those interested in understanding the intricate dynamics of cult affiliations, shedding light on the often hidden and darker side of celebrity-led cults.

Whether examining the signs of a religious cult, political cult, conspiracy theory cult, spiritual cult, new age cult, or even a celebrity or fanatical following cult, "Unveiling the Shadows" provides a comprehensive exploration of the tactics employed by these manipulative leaders. By arming oneself with knowledge, individuals can protect themselves and potentially break free from the grip of these harmful organizations.

The Dark Side of Fandom and

Fanatical Devotion: A Comprehensive Exploration

In the vast landscape of fanaticism and devotion, an often-overlooked dark side lurks, casting shadows over the unsuspecting followers. This subchapter endeavors to illuminate the hidden dangers entrenched within extreme fandom and the latent potential for cult affiliations. Regardless of whether it is religious, political, conspiracy theory-based, spiritual, new age, or celebrity-related, the signs of cult-like behavior can manifest in multifarious forms, weaving a complex tapestry of potential peril.

Signs of a Cult: Unveiling the Enigma

Cults, like insidious predators, prey on vulnerable individuals yearning for meaning, belonging, or purpose. Employing manipulative tactics such as isolation, control, and indoctrination, they ensnare their followers in a web of unwavering loyalty. Recognizing the signs of a cult becomes a critical shield, protecting individuals from the potential harm that lurks within the seemingly enticing folds of devotion.

Signs of a Religious Cult: Manipulating Belief Systems

Religious cults exploit established belief systems, often distorting traditional practices to align with their own insidious agendas. Followers may find themselves isolated from friends and family, coerced into unquestioning obedience, or unwittingly participating in harmful practices veiled under the guise of spirituality.

Signs of a Political Cult: Charismatic Leaders and Manipulation

Political cults emerge when charismatic leaders manipulate their followers' desire for societal change. Employing fear tactics, suppressing dissent, and fostering an "us versus them" mentality, they deftly blur the line between political activism and perilous fanaticism.

Signs of a Conspiracy Theory Cult: Digital Age Entrenchment

In today's digital age, conspiracy theories amass significant followings. Yet, some individuals plunge into the depths of these theories, forming cult-like communities. Rejecting mainstream information, isolating themselves from non-believers, and undergoing radicalization are common hallmarks of these digital-age cults.

Signs of a Spiritual Cult: Exploiting the Quest for Enlightenment

Exploiting individuals seeking personal growth or enlightenment, spiritual cults employ manipulation, coercion, and abuse to control their followers. Emphasizing hierarchical structures and demanding blind devotion, these groups weave a treacherous web around unsuspecting seekers.

Signs of a New Age Cult: From Enlightenment to Manipulation

New age cults allure those seeking alternative spiritual practices or self-improvement. However, they can swiftly devolve into dangerous cults when leaders exploit their followers' vulnerabilities and engage in psychological manipulation.

Signs of a Celebrity or Fanatical Following Cult: Idolization and Manipulation

Celebrity or fanatical following cults orbit around charismatic figures amassing devoted followers. Involving idolization, isolation from non-believers, and blind loyalty to the celebrity, these groups create a dangerous dynamic that can lead to manipulation and abuse.

Recognizing the signs of cult affiliations is crucial for anyone suspecting their involvement in such a group. This subchapter serves as an empowering resource, arming individuals with the knowledge to identify and comprehend the dangers lurking within the dark side of fandom and fanatical devotion. By decoding these signs, we can collectively navigate the treacherous waters of cult affiliations and reclaim our autonomy and freedom.

Breaking Free from a Celebrity Cult: A Journey to Autonomy

In the era of pervasive social media, where celebrities' lives are constantly under the spotlight, it's easy to be captivated by their glamour, talent, and seemingly perfect lifestyles. However, what if your admiration for a celebrity has metamorphosed into something more ominous? What if you find yourself ensnared in a celebrity cult?

While the notion of a celebrity cult may seem improbable, the reality is that it occurs more frequently than one might imagine. These cults wield insidious manipulation, exploiting vulnerabilities and desires for connection and validation. If you suspect you have fallen into the clutches of a celebrity cult, it is imperative to recognize the signs and take decisive steps to break free.

A key sign of a celebrity cult is an intense and obsessive fixation on a particular celebrity or public figure. This obsession can permeate your thoughts and actions, leaving little room for other aspects of your life. You might discover yourself consistently tracking their every move, emulating their style, or vehemently defending their questionable actions.

Another red flag is the presence of charismatic

leaders or influencers who act as intermediaries between the celebrity and their followers. These individuals often possess a magnetic personality, using it to manipulate and control their followers. They may create an aura of exclusivity, making you feel privileged to be part of their inner circle.

Breaking free from a celebrity cult necessitates courage and self-reflection. Begin by acknowledging that your involvement has transcended admiration, bordering on obsession. Seek support from trusted friends, family, or even professionals who can provide guidance and offer a fresh perspective.

Empowering yourself with knowledge about the tactics employed by cults is also crucial. Understanding how manipulation works will enable you to recognize the techniques being used to keep you ensnared. Remember that you have the right to think for yourself and make independent choices.

Detaching from the cult may involve distancing yourself from the celebrity's influence. Unfollow their social media accounts, limit exposure to news or gossip about them, and redirect your focus toward activities that promote personal growth and well-being.

Breaking free from a celebrity cult is a journey that demands self-reflection, support, and determination. Remember that you are not alone; others have navigated similar situations and can provide empathy and guidance. By reclaiming your autonomy and concentrating on your own life, you can liberate yourself from the grasp of a celebrity cult and regain control over your own happiness.

Nine

Recovery and Support

Recognizing and Accepting Cult Affiliation: A Comprehensive Exploration

In our intricate modern society, it is not an uncommon occurrence for individuals to find themselves ensnared within the intricate web of a cult. Be it a religious, political, conspiracy theory, spiritual, new age, or even a celebrity or fanatical following cult, the subtle signs may easily elude detection. However, unraveling these signs is paramount to breaking free from their grip and regaining control over one's life.

The initial step in recognizing and accepting cult affiliation involves educating oneself about the diverse array of cults that permeate our society. In this subchapter, we embark on a journey into the signs of various cult affiliations, shedding light on the distinctive characteristics of each. By comprehending the unique traits of religious cults, political cults, conspiracy theory cults, spiritual cults, new age cults, and celebrity or fanatical following cults, individuals can fortify themselves with the knowledge needed to identify warning signs in their own lives or the lives of loved ones.

Manifesting in various ways, signs of a cult can be elusive. In religious cults, leaders may claim a unique connection with a higher power, manipulating followers with promises of salvation and eternal reward. Political cults exploit the desire for societal change, employing mind control techniques to sway followers' beliefs and actions. Conspiracy theory cults prey on vulnerability, convincing followers they possess secret knowledge and are fighting against a powerful malevolent force. Spiritual cults promise enlightenment but often demand unwavering loyalty and financial contributions. New age cults, focusing on alternative healing methods and spiritual practices, can ensnare those seeking answers and guidance. Lastly, celebrity or fanatical following cults revolve around the worship of a charismatic figure, leading followers to blindly obey their idol's every command.

While recognizing the signs of cult affiliation can be a challenging and uncomfortable process, acceptance is the key to breaking free from their influence. Acknowledging entanglement in the web of a cult allows individuals to embark on the journey toward reclaiming autonomy and regaining control over beliefs and actions. This subchapter aspires to empower individuals with cult affiliations, providing them with the tools and knowledge needed to recognize the signs and initiate the necessary steps towards liberation.

For true crime enthusiasts, understanding the intricate workings of cults is a riveting and captivating subject. "Unveiling the Shadows: Decoding the Signs of Cult Affiliations" offers a comprehensive exploration of the signs of various cult affiliations, delving into the psychological, sociological, and historical aspects contributing to their formation and maintenance. This subchapter serves as a valuable resource for both individuals seeking personal growth and those with a general interest in unraveling the mysteries behind cult affiliations.

Overcoming Psychological Manipulation and Trauma: A Roadmap to Liberation

In the realm of cult affiliations, psychological manipulation and trauma cast ominous shadows over the lives of individuals. These insidious tactics can leave individuals feeling trapped, isolated, and vulnerable. However, there is a glimmer of hope for those who wish to break free from these destructive cycles. In this subchapter, we embark on an exploration of strategies and tools designed to help individuals overcome psychological manipulation and trauma associated with cult affiliations.

The first step in reclaiming control over one's life involves recognizing the signs of psychological manipulation. Whether entangled in a religious, political, conspiracy theory, spiritual, new age, or celebrity cult, certain red flags demand awareness. Gaslighting, isolation from loved ones, control over personal choices, and manipulation of information are common tactics employed by cult leaders. By understanding these signs, individuals can initiate the process of unraveling the web of manipulation cast upon them.

Healing from psychological trauma is a pivotal aspect of overcoming cult affiliations. Trauma can manifest in various ways, such as anxiety, depression, and post-traumatic stress disorder (PTSD). Seeking professional help from therapists or counselors specializing in trauma recovery becomes essential. They can guide individuals through the healing process, providing techniques like cognitive-behavioral therapy (CBT), eye movement desensitization and reprocessing (EMDR), and mindfulness exercises to help regain emotional well-being.

Rebuilding a support system emerges as a vital component for those who have experienced cult affiliations. Cults often isolate individuals from friends and family, making it challenging to seek help or find support. Joining support groups designed for cult survivors or reaching out to loved ones who understand one's experiences can provide a much-needed sense of belonging and validation.

Self-care practices play a significant role in overcoming psychological manipulation and trauma. Engaging in activities that bring joy, practicing mindfulness and relaxation techniques, and prioritizing mental and emotional well-being can assist in reclaiming a sense of self and building resilience.

Remember, healing is a journey, and it may take time to fully recover from the psychological manipulation and trauma associated with cult affiliations. Patience with oneself is key, and celebrating each small step toward reclaiming autonomy and freedom becomes a vital aspect of the process.

In conclusion, overcoming psychological manipulation and trauma is not only possible but achievable with the right tools and support. By recognizing the signs of manipulation, seeking professional help, building a support system, and practicing self-care, individuals can break free from the clutches of cult affiliations and regain control of their lives. In this journey, remember that you are not alone, and there is hope for a brighter future beyond the shadows of cult affiliations.

Rebuilding Personal Identity and Autonomy: A Journey of Rediscovery

One of the most arduous challenges faced by those involved in a cult is the profound loss of personal identity and autonomy. Cults exploit vulnerable individuals, manipulating their beliefs, emotions, and behaviors, ultimately causing them to detach from their authentic selves. Rebuilding personal identity and reclaiming autonomy becomes a crucial step towards healing and breaking free from the suffocating grip of cult affiliations.

Understanding the signs of cult affiliations serves as the foundational step toward regaining control over one's life. Whether ensnared in a religious, political, conspiracy theory, spiritual, new age, or celebrity cult, the signs of manipulation and control exhibit haunting similarities. Recognition of these signs empowers individuals to challenge and question their involvement, paving the way for personal growth and liberation.

The process of rebuilding personal identity commences with the rediscovery of one's values, interests, and passions outside the cult's pernicious influence. Essential to this journey is engaging in profound self-reflection and reconnecting with one's authentic self. Seeking therapy, joining support groups, or confiding in trusted friends and family members can aid in this process. By exploring personal beliefs and desires, individuals can gradually reconstruct their identity, liberating themselves from the detrimental impact of the cult.

Reclaiming autonomy necessitates the development of critical thinking skills and the cultivation of a robust sense of personal agency. Cults thrive on unquestioning loyalty and blind obedience; thus, it becomes crucial to question the beliefs and practices imposed by the cult, evaluating them against one's own values and rationality. Developing a strong sense of self-reliance and decision-making becomes paramount in regaining autonomy.

Establishing healthy boundaries and learning to say no are additional crucial steps toward reclaiming personal autonomy. Cults often exploit individuals by pressuring them into compliance with unreasonable demands and sacrificing personal boundaries. Learning to set and enforce boundaries is essential in reclaiming control over one's life and decisions.

As individuals embark on the journey to rebuild their personal identity and autonomy, seeking support from those who understand their experiences is vital. Connecting with others who have left cult affiliations or engaging with true crime enthusiasts who can empathize with the struggle is invaluable. Sharing stories, seeking guidance, and providing support can aid in the healing process, empowering individuals to regain control of their lives.

Rebuilding personal identity and autonomy is a challenging odyssey that requires courage, self-reflection, and support. By recognizing the signs of cult affiliations, reclaiming personal values, and cultivating autonomy, individuals can break free from the shadows of cult influence and rediscover their true selves. Remember, you are not alone, and there is hope for a brighter future beyond the grasp of cult affiliations.

Seeking Professional Help and Support Groups: A Roadmap to Recovery

Dealing with the complex and often traumatic experience of cult affiliations necessitates strategic steps toward recovery and healing. Whether recently leaving a cult or suspecting involvement in one, seeking professional help and joining support groups emerges as crucial components in navigating the intricate dynamics of cult affiliations.

Professional help becomes essential in understanding and addressing the intricate dynamics of cult affiliations. Therapists, counselors, and psychologists specializing in cult recovery provide a safe space to process emotions, unravel the manipulation tactics employed by cults, and help rebuild one's sense of self. These professionals assist in understanding the psychological impact of the experience, identifying any lingering trauma, and developing coping mechanisms to regain control over life.

Support groups play a vital role in the healing process by connecting individuals with firsthand knowledge of cult affiliations. Offering a non-judgmental and empathetic environment, these groups provide a platform to share stories, gain insights from others, and receive validation for experiences. The shared struggles with fellow survivors foster a sense of community, helping individuals feel understood and less isolated.

For those suspecting cult affiliations, seeking professional help and joining support groups aids in distinguishing between healthy spiritual or religious practices and potentially harmful ones. Professionals can assist in critically analyzing the signs and red flags associated with cults, enabling informed decisions about involvement.

True crime enthusiasts, interested in understanding the psychology behind cult affiliations and the motivations of cult leaders, can benefit from the expertise of professionals who have extensively studied these phenomena. Consulting with experts allows enthusiasts to gain a deeper understanding of the tactics used by cults to manipulate followers and learn about the warning signs in various types of cults, including religious, political, conspiracy theory, spiritual, new age, and celebrity or fanatical following cults.

Seeking professional help and support groups does not signify weakness but rather demonstrates strength and a commitment to reclaiming life.

Whether grappling with the aftermath of a cult experience or seeking knowledge about cult affiliations, these resources provide the tools and support needed to move forward on the path to recovery and empowerment. Remember, you are not alone, and there is hope for a brighter future beyond the shadows of cult affiliations.

Advocacy and Raising Awareness: Illuminating the Path to Empowerment

In the intricate landscape of cult affiliations, it becomes imperative to cast a spotlight on the signs and indicators that aid individuals in recognizing their involvement in such groups. The role of advocacy and raising awareness is pivotal in empowering those who suspect they have cult affiliations, fostering self-awareness, and guiding them toward reclaiming control over their lives.

This expansive subchapter, aptly titled "Advocacy and Raising Awareness," is designed to serve as a comprehensive guide and support system for individuals grappling with the complexities of cult affiliations. Its relevance extends to true crime enthusiasts fascinated by the psychological mechanisms behind cults and their followers. By delving into the unique characteristics of different cult types, readers can cultivate a thorough understanding of the signs indicative of cult involvement.

The subchapter unfolds by exploring the signs of a cult, accentuating common red flags such as charismatic leaders, isolation from family and friends, and the presence of rigid belief systems. It takes a deep dive into specific cult types, encompassing religious, political, conspiracy theory, spiritual, new age, and celebrity or fanatical following cults. Each section offers an extensive exploration of the distinct characteristics and warning signs associated with these cult categories, empowering readers to recognize these patterns in their own lives or in the lives of others.

Beyond identifying signs of cult affiliations, the subchapter underscores the critical importance of advocacy and raising awareness. It provides practical strategies for individuals to seek help, engage in open conversations, and connect with support networks that specialize in cult recovery. By fostering a proactive approach, this subchapter empowers readers to take the necessary steps toward breaking free from the clutches of cult affiliations and reclaiming their autonomy.

With its comprehensive coverage of various cult types and practical guidance, "Advocacy and Raising Awareness" stands as a beacon of hope for those ensnared in cults. Through understanding and awareness, this subchapter aims to equip readers with the knowledge and tools needed to navigate the murky waters of cult affiliations and ultimately find their way back to a life of freedom and authenticity.

Empowering Others to Escape Cult Affiliations: A Journey of Courage and Resilience

Breaking free from the suffocating grip of a cult is a formidable journey, requiring immense courage, profound self-reflection, and unwavering support from others who have navigated similar challenges. This empowering subchapter is dedicated to individuals who believe they have cult affiliations, offering valuable insights and practical steps to aid in reclaiming autonomy and rebuilding lives.

The initial step towards liberation is recognizing and comprehending the signs of cult affiliations. Whether ensnared in a religious, political, conspiracy theory, spiritual, new age, or celebrity/fanatical following cult, each presents unique characteristics. By delving into the signs of these different cult types, readers gain a deeper understanding of the manipulative techniques employed by cult leaders.

Upon identification of their involvement in a cult, individuals often face overwhelming uncertainty about how to escape. This subchapter sheds light on various strategies and resources available to facilitate the process of breaking free from the clutches of cult affiliation. It emphasizes the significance of seeking professional help, including therapists specializing in cult recovery, who can offer guidance and support during the recovery journey.

Furthermore, empowering oneself to escape a cult involves the establishment of a robust support network. The subchapter underscores the importance of connecting with others who have undergone similar experiences, as they can provide invaluable empathy, understanding, and a safe space for sharing stories. Additionally, it explores the role of family and friends in providing emotional support and assisting in the reintegration process.

To foster healing and growth, this subchapter delves into various self-empowerment techniques. It explores the power of self-reflection, aiding individuals in identifying their strengths, values, and personal aspirations. By rediscovering their true selves and cultivating a strong sense of identity, individuals can regain confidence and make informed decisions for their future.

Lastly, the subchapter offers insight into legal

and safety considerations individuals should be aware of when leaving a cult. It provides information on restraining orders, legal protection, and the importance of maintaining personal safety during the transition period.

Empowering oneself to escape a cult affiliation is a courageous and transformative journey. This subchapter serves as a comprehensive guide, aiming to equip individuals with the knowledge, resources, and support they need to reclaim their lives and move forward with newfound strength and resilience. By unraveling the shadows that shroud cult affiliations, readers can embark on their journey towards liberation and a brighter future.

Shedding Light on Cult Affiliations

The Importance of Identifying Cultic Behaviors: Safeguarding Against Manipulation and Exploitation

In our intricately woven modern society, it becomes increasingly crucial to possess an acute awareness of the signs and behaviors associated with cult affiliations. Whether one harbors suspicions of personal involvement in a cult or is merely a true crime enthusiast, understanding these red flags is paramount for protecting oneself and others from the perilous consequences of falling prey to the influence of manipulative individuals or groups.

Cults, diverse in form and structure, span the spectrum from religious and political to conspiracy theory, spiritual, new age, and even celebrity or fanatical followings. Despite these differences, they often exhibit common characteristics that serve as markers for identification. Early recognition of these signs is instrumental in thwarting the potential harm that cult involvement can inflict upon individuals and society at large.

At the forefront of cult identification is the presence of a charismatic leader wielding an extraordinary influence over their followers. Possessing a magnetic personality, these leaders employ psychological manipulation tactics to control adherents, exploiting vulnerabilities such as the desire for belonging, purpose, or answers to life's mysteries. Recognizing these influential figures and their manipulative techniques is critical for early intervention.

Another pivotal sign lies in the isolation of cult members from the external world. Cults thrive on fostering an "us versus them" mentality, actively discouraging interaction with non-members and suppressing critical thinking. This isolation establishes a perilous echo chamber where dissenting opinions are disregarded, and groupthink takes root.

Cults also frequently employ coercive tactics to maintain control. These can range from emotional and physical abuse to financial exploitation and even threats of harm to oneself or loved ones. Identifying these abusive behaviors serves as the initial step toward breaking free from the clutches of a cult and seeking assistance.

Understanding the signs associated with cultic behaviors not only empowers individuals to protect themselves and their loved ones from manipulation and exploitation but also enables true crime enthusiasts to recognize warning signs in the cases they study. This knowledge can potentially aid authorities in identifying and dismantling cults.

"Unveiling the Shadows: Decoding the Signs of Cult Affiliations" serves as an exhaustive guide to understanding the signs of various cult types. Whether one suspects involvement in a religious, political, conspiracy theory, spiritual, new age, or celebrity/fanatical following cult, this book equips readers with the necessary tools to identify and address cultic behaviors.

Through in-depth case studies, expert analyses, and practical advice, this subchapter provides readers with the knowledge needed to safeguard themselves and others. By emphasizing the importance of identifying cultic behaviors, "Unveiling the Shadows" endeavors to expose the dark underbelly of these perilous groups and contribute to a safer and more informed society.

Moving Forward and Preventing Future Cult Affiliations: A Roadmap to Empowerment

As we delve deeper into the intricate world of cult affiliations, it becomes imperative not only to understand the signs and dynamics of different types of cults but also to focus on the path forward and preventing such affiliations in the future. Whether one harbors suspicions of personal involvement in a cult or is a true crime enthusiast, this subchapter endeavors to provide actionable steps to protect oneself and others from falling into the clutches of dangerous cults.

1. Educating Yourself: Knowledge as a Shield: Cult affiliations are best combated with knowledge. By learning about the signs and tactics employed by various types of cults, individuals can fortify themselves against potential dangers. "Unveiling the Shadows: Decoding the Signs of Cult Affiliations" serves as a comprehensive guide, shedding light on the signs of religious, political, conspiracy theory, spiritual, new age, and celebrity/fanatical following cults.

2. Building Resilience: Strengthening the Core: Cults often exploit vulnerabilities and emotional needs. By fortifying emotional resilience and self-esteem, individuals create a robust foundation, making them less susceptible to the manipulations of cult recruiters. Seeking therapy or support groups aids in healing from past traumas and developing healthy coping mechanisms.

3. Cult-proof Relationships: Establishing Strong Bonds: Strong relationships with family, friends, and communities are essential for protection against cult affiliations. Cults often isolate members from loved ones, making it harder for them to leave. Maintaining open lines of communication and fostering healthy connections act as a safety net.

4. Critical Thinking: The Antidote to Manipulation: Cults frequently employ mind control techniques that erode critical thinking abilities. Training oneself to question information, conduct independent research, and critically evaluate suspicious claims helps prevent falling prey to manipulative tactics. Encouraging others to think critically creates a collective defense against cult ideologies.

5. Advocacy and Awareness: The Ripple Effect: Share knowledge and experiences with others, especially those vulnerable to cult tactics. Raising awareness about the signs and dangers of cult affiliations through social media, local community events, or support groups contributes to preventing future affiliations. The ripple effect of advocacy empowers individuals to recognize and avoid cults.

Moving forward and preventing future cult affiliations necessitates a collective effort. By educating oneself, building resilience, strengthening relationships, fostering critical thinking, and advocating for awareness, a safer and more informed society can be forged. Knowledge is power, and together, we can unveil the shadows of cult affiliations, protecting ourselves and others from their grasp.

Unveiling the Shadows: A Call to Action: Empowering Lives Through Knowledge

In the obscure recesses of society, manipulative forces clandestinely prey on vulnerable individuals, ensnaring them within the insidious grip of cult affiliations. Operating under various disguises, from religious and political to conspiracy theories, spiritual movements, and new age ideologies, these affiliations lurk in the shadows. "Unveiling the Shadows: Decoding the Signs of Cult Affiliations" is a groundbreaking book that casts a piercing light on these hidden dangers, providing empowerment for those entangled in cults and captivating true crime enthusiasts.

For those grappling with cult affiliations, this subchapter acts as a lifeline, offering a step-by-step guide to recognizing warning signs. From isolation to strict control over personal choices and suppression of critical thinking, readers are empowered to break free from the clutches of manipulative organizations and reclaim their lives.

The subchapter also caters to the insatiable curiosity of true crime enthusiasts, delving into case studies that explore high-profile cults and the devastating consequences they inflict on their followers. From the infamous Heaven's Gate to the hauntingly influential Manson Family, readers gain unparalleled insights into the inner workings of these affiliations.

Armed with knowledge and awareness, readers are emboldened to protect themselves and their loved ones from the dangers of cult affiliations. "Unveiling the Shadows: Decoding the Signs of Cult Affiliations" is a powerful tool that empowers individuals to break free from the clutches of manipulation and embark on a journey towards self-discovery and freedom. In the unveiling of these shadows, lives are transformed, and a brighter, liberated future beckons.

www.ingramcontent.com/pod-product-compliance
Lightning Source LLC
Chambersburg PA
CBHW041202150726
48006CB00016B/2077